EDITOR IN CHIEF
Miljenko Foretić

11ᵗʰ Edition

Copyright © by Matica hrvatska Dubrovnik

CIP - Katalogizacija u publikaciji
Nacionalna i sveučilišna knjižnica, Zagreb

UDK 355(4:497.13 Dubrovnik)"1991/1992"
DUBROVNIK in War / [na engleski preveli Damir
Kalogjera... [et al.] ; urednik Miljenko Foretić]. -
Dubrovnik : Matica hrvatska Dubrovnik
[etc.], 2000. - 118 str. : ilustr. 104 ; 24 cm

ISBN 953-6316-16-1

980619130

Dubrovnik in War

MATICA HRVATSKA DUBROVNIK

Dubrovnik 2002

1st edition on the occasion of the 59th P.E.N. World Congress, Dubrovnik 19–24 April 1993

Contents

5

Vlado Gotovac

The Defence of Dubrovnik

Some would like to save Dubrovnik by isolating it — by cutting its organic ties. The city is reduced to what is within its walls only: Its value is great, its beauty unique, but this is not what connects the city to a particular country and what establishes relationships with a particular community. It is a complex of the sole origin of its geographical and historical survival conditions... It has its own time, its own history — and no conditions!

Dubrovnik is to become a monument with an entirely international existence. It is to be reduced to the values that permit, justify and maintain such an existence.

An unreal monument with an unreal existence.

Its entire environment — the foundation of human survival, with all its ties — is surrendered to a different fate: a destruction from which only the city is exempt. Dubrovnik becomes an artistic composition for the sake of art, released from all earthly ties, maintained only by a pure love of beauty with no other motivation... Love is to protect the city by its geographical and historical extraterritoriality.

The remaining land around a no–man's city would be no–man's land — a ghostly and cynical outcome when a solitary value is left amidst destruction and wild barbarian fury.

Gone is the environment of Dubrovnik, which was sustained for centuries — its gardens, its villas and manor houses, regions of silence, where only chosen words, tunes and movements are used.

Gone are the arcadian intervals in the devoted and complicated concerns of the Republic.

Dubrovnik would remain like a deathly ornament.

It would survive because it turned impossible, without a purpose, incomprehensible and unreal. It would be only a decorative pin used in frozen theatricals, with an icing of gibberish.

Dubrovnik would exist only as its own magnificent gravestone, erected to the memory of its meaning — its entire homeland; a monument

7

erected to all that became incomprehensible through the city's isolation. The city itself, Croatia. Not for a moment can the texture of the city's and its homeland's fate be broken without the presence of death and deprivation of meaning. Croatia is incomprehensible without Dubrovnik, Dubrovnik is incomprehensible without Croatia. A part and the whole change roles in their common history.

Dubrovnik is the scene of great enterprises in Croatian culture, its specific national qualities and its European component parts — from its Mediterranean horizon to the historical order of stylistic expressions. During the Revival Dubrovnik was the factor that unraveled Croatia's regions like a rebellious inspiration of the country's integrity and the basic fact of its continuity. The discovery of Dubrovnik is the discovery of Croatian self–confidence at work. It is the mutual influence of city and Homeland — when their fate is explained.

Dubrovnik has lived the surrounding conditions and effects of its survival both organically and symbolically. Its environment is not only a working or useful suburb. It is organized like a complex of the historical survival which protected itself by walls in a logical and deliberate manner, never breaking up the spacial continuum of common industry and living conditions. Within and without the walls the city governs, as well as its order, and the logic of its community. From Ston to Konavle the community is expressed in various ways. The city's history can be seen everywhere.

Therefore has Dubrovnik been reduced to its walls — an Etruscan scene: a magnificent monument in a dead landscape. It is a symbol without the sense that makes it a living history, a symbol as testimony to the greatness of that which has vanished.

Such a protection in death is the aim of those who consider the abandonment of Croatia as a compensation for the beauty of Dubrovnik. Incredible trading with obscenity and death. Cynicism and murder are presented as solidarity with an aesthetic greatness. The abandonment of Croatia is an imminent murder of Dubrovnik. The city can be preserved only with its homeland. The city is its homeland's reality. The homeland is the city's unconditioned foundation.

Dubrovnik has been created with the Croatian sense of measure: no false pretences, no fake facts — all its proportions have come about with a vow to virtue, with its discipline and beauty. The state of affairs is acknowledged, because it does not halt dreams faithful to the horizons of the city's spirit. Like a golden motto of light stands the ancient Croatian church above Dubrovnik, where from time to time the East

8

and the West lead a dialogue in tropes, figures, inexpressible phantasies...

Contrary to all this is the barbarian monomania, a demonic lack of history, a right to everything, founded on a substitution of Christ's love by the sacrament of hate conceived in the devotion to saint Sava.[1] The prophetic spirit, lonely, without action as a limit, with hands untied in the denial of Other. This is what the environment of Dubrovnik is relinquished to, this is what Croatia is surrendered to, in order to uphold the beauty of the city by death.

In the empty space created by such a death Great Serbia would stand as a sentinel — as the last instance of respect for the international opinion... marked by nonsense.

The simplicity of the barbaric axe and its blows in a park, in a sign of the history of enigmatic paths, whose routes are interpreted through dreams and imagination... aimed at the prosperity of a world. — Gardens of meditation, for example; gardens of love, kept with pleasure (and mostly with taste), sensuous gardens, peaceful gardens, recreating the power of triviality and greatness at the same time.

The rambling diversities confronted by a barrier come to a halt. The great pragmatists of our days make sentimental gestures, justifying their confusion and repeated nonsense of their charities. Those who are saved must often abandon the reasons and values attached to their tragedies and thus continue their existence in a formless state. Practical help deprives them of a horizon full of dreams!

This is the pragmatism of modern Europe, modern America, modern Japan. The pragmatism of an economic and technological hegemony and its conditions. It is a question of who rules the world. It is not posed as an ideological question, as a futurological question of some idealist — it is only a question of how economic power can be successfully developed. It belongs to a complacent realm of production and consumption.

Its aim is a pragmatic release of every charge of an epoch marking change that began by the breakdown of totalitarianism.

Dubrovnik is a sentimental detail of that effort. The scandalous inadequacy is first and foremost due to the fact that it does not contain conditions of the breakdown of our regional ideology — of Yugoslavism. For a pragmatic eye everything in the detail is reduced to the preser-

---

*   Medieval Serbian statesman, the first Serbian episcopus and national saint.

vation of an oasis of beauty against tribal furies which are tearing apart their common totalitarian state in the turmoil of war, instead of bringing democracy to it peacefully.

Banality appears as superiority of pragmatism to the revivalist ideals of nations. The space between self–sufficiency, a decadently pathetical neuroticism, and the cold insensitivity of politics... is entirely inadequate for the tragical dimension of a return to history and to geographical maps, of nations long forgotten, hidden, and repudiated.

Croatia is at this moment an absolute opposition to the great pragmatism. It is tragically obsessed with ideals which are the conditions for the establishment of her place in the world. The scenes are full of blood and upheaval, all the fury of revolution and breakdown, of adventure, fell upon Croatia in Great Serbia's rage...

Dubrovnik has been hit by the sentimentality of pragmatism. In the name of beauty, but in a trivial manner. Incapable of comprehending the whole, of comprehending its context and meaning, it ignores even the suburban landscape. They do not know how to employ Dubrovnik when it is saved, where to employ it, for what purpose — a Dubrovnik dismantled of all organic matter. Dubrovnik can exist in harmony with its beauty only if Croatia exists — because Croatia is a condition for Dubrovnik's existence.

From a pragmatical point of view it is incomparably easier to save Dubrovnik in isolation than in a perspective and with the ties of its whole survival. Nobody's Dubrovnik is a toy for international safekeeping, a Croatian Dubrovnik is a logical fact and a majestic scene of beauty exposed to the threat of barbaric invasion.

Serbia can appear on the Mediterranean only over its ruins, remaining equally far away from them as from what they stood for. The destruction of Dubrovnik by the Serbs is not an expression of longing for light, for the South, for a world of clarity and reality. No pilgrimage. On the contrary! It is a will to own, to destroy, a will of resentment. This is why they would consent to a dead Dubrovnik, to a city reduced to a scenery for their stage. They want Croatia to be a no–man's land. But this is possible only if the marks of our history disappear from our land. Then only can they colonize it — a deserted, formless province of Great Serbia.

Dubrovnik is no exception in this programme. Its role is to witness, with its deathly loneliness the city's beauty is meant to explain the desolation of Croatia as a whole.

The fate of Croatia is the knot of this moment. The future tied up in it takes on the greatness of the past and with it its foundation as well as its freedom. The doors open to a new adventure coming from its native ground, the coastline. A knot of a planetary revolution moving away from totalitarianism. A knot of a regional revolution moving away from Yugoslavism. Our entire history comes to self–awarenes in the knot, finds an explanation for the sublime adversity, grown to such dimensions as would be incomprehensible without credibility, without modesty and without taking a resolute view of the future. It is a greatness growing with the future of the world, still unknown but inseparably linked with the power of the past.

This is how Dubrovnik is defended: as a place where Croatia becomes the world's turning point in front of a yet unimaginable adventure — Croatia of the Mediterranean, Croatia of Central Europe, Croatia of Byzantium and Islam — the only European country formed in this manner, as a triple braid, special, integral, unique. What is gathered in Croatia is turned into its novelty, its authenticity. And all this is defended in Dubrovnik.

It is impossible to preserve the complex of Dubrovnik by an international sentimental game, which is only a pragmatically devised stand–by refuge. Those who admire Dubrovnik outside its historical and geographical horizons, where its foundations and its context lie, have reached a tourist and cultural point of moral agitation, where conciliation of their own relations is required, but no concern about anything else — that is to say about the unity of historical conditions and their meaning.

Perhaps it is not cynical self–content, perhaps it is only individuality, permanently matched with occasions of joy, of content, of the magic mountain.

Dubrovnik defended in this manner is only a frozen picture of the Croatian soul. It is kept still like a decoration and as a substitute for tragedy. Incredible.

Translated by Dora Maček

Slobodan Prosperov Novak

Theorem about the Egg

The book "A year of Croatian national customs" by M. Gavazzi has had an impact in this country comparable to the one Fraser's Golden Bough had had in the world in the early 20th century. Indeed, current and ancient ethnological and folklore observation has been very rich with us and there exist copious studies and monographs in the field. The study of customs is not attractive only to those who want to learn about them but it has become a reliable corroboration to those who would like to use it to test the great theories and praxis of the present which is characterized by a crisis of intellect in the first place.

You couldn't have led me to a greater temptation than ask me to write a contribution for this war–number of the periodical Dubrovnik about Easter, about its symbolism which always suggests that Easter is *something more.* Surrounded by eggs one is tempted to begin *ab ovo.* As, according to the order of things, at the beginning there was the word and life was in it, for the study of customs, one could say, that at the beginning there was the egg and that life was in it. In this most exciting of human topics, in the egg — the most perfect form in the universe known to us — in the loneliness of its shell and its unrepeatedness, in one of the greatest solitudes of the universe, the membrane, in its simulation of the universe, a most peculiar meeting of life and death of the subtlest quality takes place.

The analysis of this symbol, and the egg is one of the most ambiguous symbols that we know of, accommodating it in the context of Easter, the greatest mystery of our civilization, is a kind of task which every now and then gets caught up in ambiguity. This symbol is linked to the lent but at the same time it is orientated towards the exit from it and by its direction it helps us to face the major riddle of our existence: the setting up of the relation between nature and history. There exists in the world internal link of the phases in nature and moments of history in the framework of which human life lasts. This coordination is equal to the one of the day and night, between dawn and dusk, equinox and solstice.

There is no division between nature and human history which in some periods was stated in the sense that nature was cyclic and that human history was developing and advancing. No, that is not true and nowadays we are more aware than ever that nature is not a given objective reality, a domain for scientific research, but that nature is the most important component in the dramatic happening of man. The nature is the domain which is interpreted by means of myths to which a person comes into contact via rites. I had to state this banal truth because in our midst there is little awareness that as distinguished from ideologized sociological, politological and philosophical disciplines, the circles of the Croatian folkloristic and ethnological studies have reached the peaks of scholarly achievement, and as it is usual to put it today, the European levels.

Once I have said that I must take a step further and add that Croatian Easter eggs, the Easter eggs from the parts where they will not be brought to the dinner table this Easter, suggest to me that these symbols could not be interpreted from the outside. They could be interpreted only by entering them, by living them in their inside. Rites, customs, festivals do not belong to the horizon of the rational. On the contrary, they belong to the emotional, irrational and mysterious. We have enough of the superficial interpreters of our reality, we are fed up with those who are not prepared to penetrate inside the phenomena, who are not prepared to enter deeper into anything, who do not want to see social life in its deeply entrenched collective balance. In Croatia, to which every fundamentalism should be unacceptable since she just emerged from one, the experience of the customs and their antiquity should be recognized as a miracle of Christianity, a miracle expressed in the Christian Calendar totally in keeping with the feeling of the people and individuals, closely linked with the dialectics of that feeling like family Christmas, the eruptive Carneval, the Lent of sadness, the autumn of the dead and the summer of happiness. That should be the folklore of our everyday life and not the Mrduša Donja* of our mentalities and small information.

May I remind you in connection with the symbol of the egg, that in its shape something most beautiful is hidden. That is because the egg carries potentiality. It is not an organism as yet. It is restless and therefore one of the most delicate things we know. Its shell is transparent and like each beginning it issues light to the outside. There is something in the egg which can remind us of the reality we live in, something

---

*   "Hamlet at Mrduša Donja" is an important play by Brešan. (1936)

that can offer some advice to those who would be prophets of that reality but are incapable of it. The fact is that as much as the egg is perfect, the birth is not. The very imperfectness of the birth is a proof of the perfectness of the egg, it is the proof of its holy symbolism. But Easter, and one has to emphasize that today, cannot be imperfect. There are no imperfect Easters, there are no unhappy Easters as they wanted to suggest when they called on us to celebrate past Easters. There are not and neither could be past Easters. Easter never was: It only may be! Only a poor and deranged mind may seek in the cycles of nature the calendar marking of the days which happen to be important to him.

The greatest threat to the revival of Croatia is primitivism which unfortunately we come across too often even in the holy domains and over the holy topics and contents of our country. The queries are coming from abroad asking whether we are becoming right–wing and what is happening with us anyway. They could have asked us, for that matter, whether we are becoming left–wing. Their question would be equally imprecise. The problem of our direction and turns unfortunately is not a horizontal one. It is a vertical problem, it is the problem of the lowering of the level. Even at her most holy spots Croatia is lowering her levels. Therefore in these days at the eve of the holiday of the rise, on the eve of the holiday of the greatest of all mysteries, it should be said, and I am going to end with it, indeed, I am going to end with the egg. The Easter egg will arrive to this long suffering country in the hands of our soldiers, in the hands of the generation which alone can guarantee a future to Croatia. It is that generation that will fully understand (since things like that can only be understood from inside and seen only from inside the shell) and recognize who in these fateful hours for Croatia are tired roosters and plucked hens and who are those who can offer Croatia a programme of on Easter 1992 and Renewal.

Easter 1992

Translated by Damir Kalogjera

Božidar Violić

Harshness vs. Harmony

I constantly see the silhouette of Croatia on television. It's a bird. At the top of one of its wings is Vukovar, and at the end of the other is Dubrovnik. And there, they stepped on our wings, and there they grounded us. The beak in Istria, and the heart in Zagreb.

We did not believe this would happen. We thought that it was not possible. It seemed to be completely unthinkable even as an idea. Now, when it has happened, there is no need to reproach one another. It's unnecessary and ugly. A reproach offered after the fact is poor consolation for the pain endured and the quarrels will not diminish the unhappiness and suffering. The fear is still alive in wide–open eyes. Let's be still, let's pull ourselves together, let's examine our guilt in silence, everyone for themselves, this will bring us closer together because the guilt is a common one, and the helplessness is general, surpassing shame at all levels. If we had done, I don't know what, if we knew and could have done something, the outcome would not have been any different. Dubrovnik had to be besieged and scarred by destruction. When the assault began, it was already too late, everything had been lost long ago. Defeat was inevitable, inscribed as fate within the lines of its centuries–old beauty, easily marred, and indefensible. And we would lean on this beauty, God! We saw in it the untouchable pledge of peace, a holy shield guaranteeing security and salvation. We were overly naïve, displaying such unguardedness that even God would not believe it to be genuine.

The horrors of the war, like a Great Tremor, rocked the foundations of the City, uncovering the sad reverse side of our thoughtlessness. In the flames of the blaze, the polish of attractiveness which for decades we had been applying to the stern, stone walls, and the wounded façades revealed the tragic face of Dubrovnik. The superficiality of our infatuation has been exposed, the enemy proved to us in a daring and cynical way, before the face of the world, that his hatred is more sincere and profound than our declaration of love. Behind a torn–up postcard, the City surfaced as distant and utterly abandoned. At once, it became

15

clear that it had been alone for a long time, and that for years, it had lived misunderstood, in an unhappy marriage with its inhabitants and neglected by its extended family, pushed into a pretty but faded memento of an entire nation.

The indisputable fact that we were not aware of before this war is that Dubrovnik was neglected. The most tragic thing is that the Dubrovnik people themselves were not aware of this. As it usually is in life, only when disaster strikes — and a bigger disaster could not have struck us — do you begin to come to your senses, does every person go through introspection. If I were to be sadly optimistic, I would say that the most valuable consequence to come out of what happened is the knowledge of how deeply Dubrovnik, through its past, its culture and beauty is tied to Croatia. As a result, I feel even more my own share of guilt in the tragic aftermath of mutual non–recognition. The concept of our whole (possible) future, meaning co–existence, should be based on the recognition of our fatal mutuality. The greatness of the love between Romeo and Juliet revealed itself at the moment of their forced separation. When Romeo was expelled from Verona, the audience of the tragedy perceived the magnitude of their connection shown through suffering and death.

We did not understand the beauty of Dubrovnik, we were blind to its very meaning, "we forgot the soul" which was left to us by Count Ivo as a warning. The beauty of Dubrovnik is aristocratic, its core is haughty and delicate, enclosed within the whiteness of a carved seashell. From outside, it looks cold and unapproachable, and its appearance reminds us of its origins. The gentry imbued into the core the dignity and finesse of the Dubrovnik gentleman which has still not died out in the blood of the illegitimate children. And we were legally trading its heritage, selling its prints, taking advantage of it for an easy life, fancy and expensive, which was so worthless that it was shameful. In our cowardly minds, we expected that after all this, Dubrovnik would serve as a refuge from warfare, would exclude us, with our unquestioned pedigree, from the horrors which descended upon unlucky regions of Croatia. We could not understand in the bad times just as we could not in the good times. Had we been able to perceive its soul, we would have understood that the refinement of its shape had to be hurt, and the nobility of its structure, maimed, and the finesse of the carved stone, chipped.

The beauty of Dubrovnik is a sublime announcement of the spiritual integrity of the Croats, of the hundred–year old energy of their imagination, collected and preserved for all eternity. Dubrovnik is our Eter-

Damir Viličić / Stradun during the fiercest shelling, December 6, 1991

Pavo Urban / Shelling of the Stradun in the early morning, December 6, 1991

Miro Kerner / Dubrovnik in flames, December 6, 1991

Miro Kerner / Shelling of Hotel »Belvedere«, November 12, 1991

Miro Kerner / Shelling of Pile and Hotel »Imperial«, November 12, 1991

**_Miro Kerner_ / Burnt–out house in the street Široka ulica,
December 6, 1991**

KATEGORIZACIJA OŠTEĆENJA NA OBJEKTIMA OŠTEĆENIM
RATNIM RAZARANJEM STARE GRADSKE JEZGRE DUBROVNIKA
Listopad - Studeni - Prosinac 1991.

REPUBLIKA HRVATSKA
ZAVOD ZA ZAŠTITU SPOMENIKA KULTURE I PRIRODE
DUBROVNIK

**Categorization of buildings damaged by war actions against the
Old Town nucleus of Dubrovnik (October, November, December
1991)**

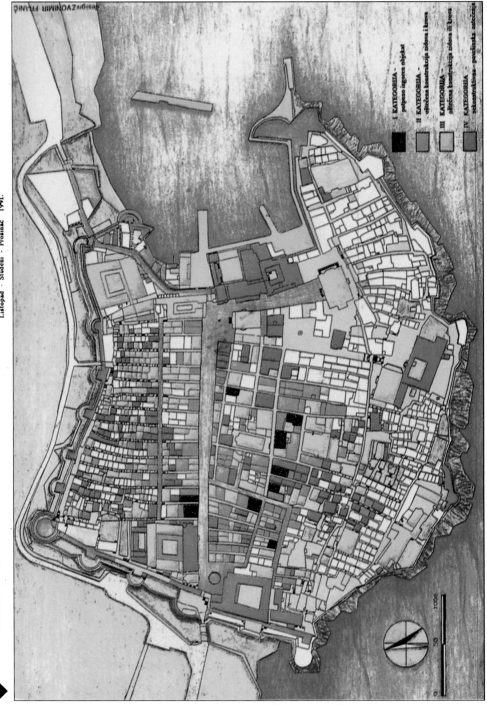

Sites of damage on buildings resulting from war ravages in the Old Town nucleus. (October – November – December 1991)

Damir Viličić / **Shelling of the Old City Harbour, December 6, 1991**

Miro Kerner / House in flames in the street Široka ulica,
December 6, 1991

Pavo Urban / The Port is ablaze — the Old City Harbour, November 1991

Pavo Urban / **The Old City Harbour in flames, November 1991**

Damir Fabijanić / Interior of a house — the Mansion Martinušić, St. Joseph street, December 6, 1991

Zvekovica and the Bay of Župa — February 1992

Destroyed and burnt–out Zvekovica — February 1992

Miro Kerner / Damage on the Dominican Monastery, December, 6, 1991

nal City. Its beauty is transcendental which is why it eludes us at every moment, it is always with us, in us, and is present in the decades before us. If some non–existent world force had restricted our enemies regarding the scene of their crimes to only one city, they would have selected Dubrovnik. To kill Croatia's soul. Every strike against the City causes us deadly pain. But we remember that its soul is immortal.

The beauty of Dubrovnik has been transformed into "harmony" (skladnost). The word derives from Dubrovnik and it expands the meaning of beauty, the notion of beauty, enriches it and adds its own character. No language (as far as I know) has this word with the meaning it has in Dubrovnik. The Dubrovnik "skladnost" means not only refinement but also the connection the people have with the scenery and architecture of the City. The special link among the three fundamental levels of life (so rare in the world) is still alive in Dubrovnik — the level of Man, the level of City, and the level of Nature. The People, the City and the scenery of Dubrava (Dubrovnik's nickname) are intertwined in harmony which is then transferred to the inhabitants of the City and leaves its mark on every Resident. A pretty girl in Dubrovnik is called "skladna", this not only means she's physically attractive, but also that she has her own harmony with her surroundings, with both the City and the landscape.

And the adjective, beautiful, "lijep", which I have heard in conversational speech, is in Dubrovnik used with unbelievable nouns, creating meanings that are found nowhere else. Dubrovnik people even take it into the realm of taste, and they sometimes say for soup or grilled fish that it is beautiful, but they are not talking about how it looks, they are referring to its delicious flavor. I found it funny at first to hear people refer to fritters as "beautiful", but later I thought about the experience of beauty melting in your mouth and I took it seriously with poetic connotations. Similarly, harsh means ugly (in the whole of Dalmatia), but the notion of harshness as brutality and crudeness lingers. Therefore, harshness is ugliness and harshness in one word, that is, harsh ugliness or ugly harshness. When juxtaposed with harmony, I detect a subtext of conflict before the walls of Dubrovnik, a layered meaning. Harshness vs. harmony.

A specific character to the war around Dubrovnik is given by the relation between the inability to attain beauty and beauty which cannot defend itself against raging inability. Those wishing to destroy harmony with harshness expose their own tragic position. Not only do they know that they do not possess it, but they can clearly feel that they will be unable to attain it in their lifetimes. The root of their hatred lies in the desperation, envy and bitterness which they feel towards shape, purity and beauty which is not theirs, and cannot nor will ever be theirs. Destruction is the only way left to them — a hopeless consolation which is extinguished each time the devastation stops.

If politicians were to think beyond the framework of their pragmatic goals, they would understand that irrational drives lie beneath this war. Because, someone who considers Dubrovnik to be their town will never try to destroy it. A man cannot destroy beauty which he thinks of as his own. If someone truly believes that Dubrovnik is his town, it is out of the question that he would torch it and destroy it with so much hatred, especially when it is a town of such exceptional beauty representing a valuable heritage not only for us but also for the whole world. The world itself is beginning to understand that this is an authentic European town with its own harmony, with its own tradition and past. When someone destroys such a town, every politician in the world, if he thinks psychologically, (and this means as a sensitive human being), will comprehend at the very start of contemplation that the person who destroys a town doesn't love it, and that this town is not his own. The ferocity by which the attacks were conducted are the best indicator that this was never his town, nor could it, after its devastation, become his town. Nevertheless, Serbia is stubbornly trying to conquer Croatian land and is even trying to convince itself and others that it is liberating it. However, the manner in which its Army is conducting its conquests is completely unknown in the history of warfare. Serb conquerors carry out frenzied attacks like a retreating army embittered by defeat. In their advances, they use reprisal tactics, and destroy before them what other armies usually destroy upon their retreat. The wartime madness seems to have distorted the aim of conquering, they did not notice that the basic motivation of the aggression had become subordinate to a strategy of hatred. It was not even a month before the masks of political pretence fell away transforming the war into as a callous war crime.

I have been paralyzed by the horror. As a boy, I lived through the Italian occupation, and I don't remember that even with my eyes widened by fear, saw such terrible destruction and arson back then. The Italians did not destroy Split, nor did they force us to leave our homes because we were Croats. Not a stone of Diocletian's Palace was chipped, as they were convinced that it was theirs and wanted to preserve it for themselves forever. In the Balkan siege of Dubrovnik, there is no trace of such an outsiders' wish for possession. Instead, there is a driving brotherly need to destroy, instinctive and blind, which has been inherited together with the need to plunder. Our attackers of today are themselves besieged, crazed by their own ugliness. Otherwise, why would they with so much heroic passion desecrate the beauty which they are thinking of seizing? When a man wishes for a beautiful woman to be his forever, he won't poke out her eyes during the courtship.

The disagreement between the Dubrovnik region and its Balkan surroundings has been going on for decades: it is disharmony between "a growth" of beauty and an area of ugliness which surrounds it. Sooner or later, it had to lead to such a tragic conflict. As time passed, it became clearer that the beauty was elusive and the harmony became prominent among all its surroundings. The beauty even elevated itself above the very residents of the town and the country it belongs to. The solitude of Dubrovnik's harmony began decades before this war: much earlier, a raw and primitive mentality with different political ideas began to draw harmony away from the beauty. This mentality never understood it and had no sensibility for it. But previous misunderstanding cannot lessen the criminal guilt of the attackers of today on the City, rather it points to its background, to the roots of envy embedded in the "genius" of the Balkan barbarians. A dirty man cannot tolerate cleanliness. Cleanliness only insults him, showing him how dirty he is. The only thing such a man can do (since it would never occur to him to shower) is to retaliate by soiling the beauty.

When a man used to bathing and living in light loses his water and light, inner feelings of cleanliness and illumination are strengthened. The sense of a deeply rooted desire for light and cleanliness grows and multiplies in geometrical proportion to the level of humiliation and material loss suffered. Maybe we would never know how pure the water is and how much our cleanliness requires the purity of water if they had not taken the water away from us. I'm not expecting the "other side" to understand this, but I cannot surpress my need to compare this siege with the conquering of Dubrovnik by Napoleon. It never occurred to Napoleon, that is, to his Marshal Marmont, later "the Duke of Dubrovnik", to take water away from the City. Because he did not come to conquer Dubrovnik in order to remove its cleanliness but to add another clean city to his large French Empire. The City of cleansed harmony giving off the light gathered from the sun. Conquering was never a peace–loving phenomenon but who the conqueror is can be seen by the conquering. Dubrovnik could turn over the keys of the city to Marmont but it will not surrender to this army made up of "dukes of opanci" (Serbian moccasins) because cleanliness cannot be surrendered to dirtiness, nor can harmony collapse before harshness. This is a collision between two mutually exclusive worlds, which are not joined in life or death.

19

I'm not consoled by the saying that reason wins in the end. I don't know where I would begin with this reason that emerges at the end of bloody madness, even if it emerges as a winner. It reminds me of a life insurance policy which is never big enough, even in the proper hands. Despite reason, the end of the war is still far off and real peace is even farther away. The stillness and serenity of life in harmony appeared to have abandoned us forever, running to the end of the world. I am not looking forward to a peace which brings about only an end to the killing, it will disperse my fear but it can't save me from despair.

. . .

I refuse to accept the wisdom of experience which teaches us that "time heals all wounds". I don't want my wound to heal. For as long as I live, I will see to it personally that my wound is not healed by time, I will live with it until the end. Not because of masochism or vain spite but in an attempt to defend reason. Only an open wound can justify injured beauty, can bring back balance to disturbed harmony. Without our grief, it is lost forever.

. . .

We should not seek revenge, this is forbidden by our upbringing and our beliefs. I shall use reason only to stop my hatred and revenge. If I succeed in this, I will consider this a victory of reason and the supreme extent of my humaneness. I shall contain myself in the name of the European Mediterranean where I was born and raised. But I will not forget. This time, we must not forget. I am saying this to myself, repeating it to myself all the time, and I would like for others to remember as well: we mustn't forget even one cypress tree because we will plant new ones in its name only!

Translated by Kathy Ann Ladun

Ivo Banac

Dubrovnik and Vukovar

Vukovar and Dubrovnik. Two prongs of Croat anguish. It is as if their history is being repeated. The Vuka River, which suggested the name of the medieval fortress of Vukov, present–day Vukovar, was cited by the ancients as Ulca fluvius, precisely in connection with the raid of Moesian legate Calcina Severus against the natives. From 1377 to 1382 Vukovar was held by Ivan Horvat, the banus of Mačva, the same Ban Ivaniš who will later, as an opponent of Emperor Sigismund, break from the Usora toward Vukovar in alliance with Serbian prince Lazar Hrebeljanović. We know practically nothing about Vukovar under the Turks, but after the liberation, in 1687, it became, in time, the center of the County of Srijem.

General Kadijević's *People's Army* of 16 November 1991 seeks to explain the failures and the prolonged campaign of the so–called Yugoslav People's Army (JNA) at Vukovar as a result of concern for "the Serbs in captivity". This sad tabloid, which was until recently full of notices offering exchanges of officers' apartments from across Croatia, consoles itself with the thought that soon the "elite shock troops of our army" will unfurl the "Yugoslav tricolor in the center of free Vukovar". But the truth — and at the same time irony — is that the tricolor with the red star was buried forever precisely in the city in which the Communist Party of Yugoslavia (KPJ) was born. It should be remembered that Vukovar was the site of that congress of the KPJ which in Communist historiography bore the name of Second or Vukovar Congress, but was in fact the first congress of Yugoslav Communists, because at this congress the party adopted its name, program, statute, as well as twenty–one conditions for accession into the Comintern. It was from this congress that Serbian party boss Sima Marković wrote to his old comrade Ilija Milkić in Moscow with news that the "regional party princes (his name for the Croat and Slovene oppositionists) grumbled against the centralization (of the party) more than anything else". Marković ended up in Stalin's Gulags, Serbian centrist Živko Topalović graduated to the wartime headquarters of collaborationist Chetniks

21

(and later in emigration in London), and Croat oppositionists Bornemissa and Brudniak ended their days as socialist retirees.

In 1919 and 1920 Vukovar had a powerful Communist organization with two newspapers — *Workers' Sentinel* and satirical *Brambles*. Its red circle produced Josip Cazi, trade union official, and Bogomir Herman, who under the pseudonym A. B. C. initiated, in 1933, the "conflict of the Left", aiming his attack squarely at Miroslav Krleža, Croatia's greatest writer and Communist dissident. From Vukovar, too, moreover on May Day 1991, marched that ominous unit of Croatian policemen into the ambush of Borovo Selo and martyrdom. Vukovar is, figuratively, the beginning and the end of a movement and a state. It began with the song that glorified labor, with the claim on the pages of *Workers' Sentinel* that such things were accomplished in the course of the First World War that "neither (Croatian king) Krešimir, nor (Serbian Emperor Stefan) Dušan the Powerful could accomplish... The South Slavs, for the first time in their existence, are faced with the task of founding a great, strong, and lasting unitary state". And it ended with massacre and the ninth scene from the pages of Belgrade's oppositional journal *Time*: "People are coming out of basements, stunned, frightened, broken. None of the civilian Serbs claimed to be a hostage, and we asked all. All remained (in Vukovar) in hope that it would not come to this, but nobody, they say, held them against their will. On Monday, 18 November, we look at a column of 2, 000 people as they are boarding buses. All are Croats. Nobody knows where they are being taken."

I do not wish to speak of Vukovar with pathos or lachrymosely. Vukovar is a great sign (and a caesura) in Croatian history. Just as the Ottoman wars remain in the sign of Sziget, not Sisak or Slankamen, so, too, this war of liberation will remain in the sign of Vukovar. Perhaps a new Pavao Ritter Vitezović is already writing a Vukovar epitaph similar to the Sziget memorial to Nikola Šubić Zrinski:

> Stand and read descreetly, comprehend and weep,
>   it is a sin to tread on this tomb.
> There has not been since the dawn of this world
>   anybody more worthy, who has merited more tears
> than this tomb, which holds a wonder of this world,
>   a figure of living faith, a flower of martial bloom.

Vukovar is not our Stalingrad or Alcazar. It is only and uniquely Vukovar, a wonder of Croat bravery and will, even when the youth of Paris introduce new signs at the "Stalingrad" Metro station that bear the name of our Vukovar.

And Dubrovnik? It would take us far afield should we attempt to mention even the best–known facts about this city of Croatian Muses. This is the city in which Ilija Crijević (Aelius Lampridius Cervinus) wrote his seductive Latin odes, the city of the lady for whom Šišmundo Menčetić withered, the city of stern Dom Mavro Vetranović and funloving Dom Marin Držić, the city in which Nikola Božidarević painted his self–portrait on the sword of St. Martin in the church of Our Lady of Danče, the city to which Mihajlo Hamzić brought the plastic modes of Andrea Mantegna, the city of buoyant baroque verse of Ivan Gundulić and Junije Palmotić, the city of Ignjat Đurđević's hymn to the newborn Christ — the dread of Hell, the city of Ruđer Bošković's first encounter with the starry firmament, the city of Ivo Vojnović's "Sonnets of Lapad" and his state–building enthusiasms ("this is a state — state... and all else is re'âyâh, mere Turkish slaves"), the city of Frano Supilo's youth and his "Conversation on the Main Street" from *Red Croatia*. But, there was always, too, an opposition to Dubrovnik as the symbol of culture — Antun Gustav Matoš's and Miroslav Krleža's hostility to "Ragusation" and supposed Dubrovnik opportunism. To this day Dubrovnik is demonstrating the untruth of such false accusations.

Proofs existed even before, because the Republic of Dubrovnik sought peace only up to a well–defined point. It is well to remember here two giants of an earlier Dubrovnik martyrdom — Marojica Kabužić and Nikolica Bunić. In 1667 Dubrovnik was destroyed in the so–called Great Earthquake, which halved the population and seriously upset the republic's patrician administration and state independence. That was a time still more somber than Milošević's and Kadijević's autumn of 1991. That was a time when the historian Ivan Lucić and churchman and polyhistor Stijepo Gradić, both residents of Rome, walked the banks of the Tiber in tears. Some ten years after the earthquake, when Dubrovnik still was on its knees, the Ottoman Grand Vezir Merzifonlu Kara Mustafa Pasha decided to seek new tribute from Dubrovnik and, should the Republic not be able to pay, to subject it to blockade and, finally, to occupation. In anticipation of these demands, the Senate of the Republic of Dubrovnik sent Kabužić and companions to the Great Vezir in Istanbul, and Bunić to the pasha of Bosnia. They were instructed to defend the liberty of their country and not to accept any excessive terms. Kara Mustafa threw Kabužić into a plague–infested prison for ordinary criminals. The Bosnian pasha had Bunić chained and taken to the Silistria fortress, on the Danube.

The two ambassadors did not yield even in gravest distress. All pressures and attempts to break them were answered with the words "*Non possumus* — We cannot.*" Tormented and weakened, Nikolica Bunić died in chains in Silistria on 16 August 1678. Marojica Kabužić was freed soon thereafter, because the war with Russia forced Kara Mustafa to turn his eye from his Ragusan prisoner. The government of Dubrovnik, which was always hostile to the glorification of any individual, nevertheless decided to commemorate the loyalty of Bunić with a plaque in the Council's building. This temple of Dubrovnik's statehood was torn down under the Austrian administration in the nineteenth century, but the plaque still hands in the new neoclassicist Town Hall, though on a wall that is hidden from view, at the entrance. When you visit Dubrovnik, and we shall all soon visit it, do not fail to take a look at this humble plaque. It is worthwhile to cite its text, which I am translating from Latin:

D. O. M.
To Nikola Bunić the son of Ivan
the senator of exceptional prudence
who in the most difficult times for the Republic
took upon himself a trying legation to the neighbouring viceroy
of Bosnia
and then was sent by him by force to the Emperor of the Turks
at Silistria
where, after a long captivity, he died for the liberty of the fatherland,
having merited by his death and the constancy of his soul
the immortality of name for all posterity.
This monument was erected by the decision of the Senate
in honor and memory in the year 1678.

The Dubrovnik sense for common good, which is the essence of politics, can be felt on every bit of Dubrovnik land from Pelješac to Prevlaka. The best evidence of this is the ceremony of the unfurling of the flag of St. Blaise, the patron of Dubrovnik, on 3 February, the Saint's feastday. This was the privilege of the Admirals of the fleet, who were by tradition from the island of Lopud. Lujo Vojnović gave an admirable description of this event in his memoirs of Lopud: "On the feastday of St. Blaise, arrayed in the scarlet damask fabric, (the admiral) would unfurl the Saint's standard and simultaneously shout into the four winds the hallowed formula of joy in the rare moments of gaiety and unconcern of the tormented state: "Life and victory, peace and prosperity to this most serene and most exalted Republic of Dubrovnik.

May God protect it and hold it for many years on the land and the sea!"
And the people responded: 'Long live St. Blaise on the land and the
sea!' "

I do not doubt for a moment that Dubrovnik is earmarked for life and
victory, peace and prosperity, and, for us, that is Croatia. It is not earmarked for bondage, which the enemy army announced in a leaflet
addressed to "Ustaša criminals" that it dropped over Dubrovnik. Nor
shall I comment on the writing of various "experts," who at the time
of Dubrovnik's agony demonstrated the extent of their commitment to
truth and justice.

Instead, let me note that Dubrovnik and Croatia are earmarked for the
prophecy of Gundulić. You will remember that Gundulić in his *Osman*
speaks how Dubrovnik offered refuge to the Serbian Despot Đurađ
Branković, who fled to Dubrovnik ahead of the Turks, an act of mercy
that provoked the wrath of Sultan Murat:

> But Murat, when he heard
> that Despot Đurađ took his gold
> and then went to Dubrovnik
> where he is protected in freedom
>
> quickly sent his messengers
> to the radiant city of Dubrovnik,
> sending gifts to the rector and council
> that they give up Đurađ to his power;
>
> or otherwise, he threatened,
> in a bloody fierce battle
> that he will subject their city
> to his imperial flaming sword.
>
> But Dubrovnik, amidst serenity
> in which it gained liberty's crown,
> despite golden bribes and threats
> remained steadfast in its faith;
>
> so that the same haughty Sultan
> in surprise, exclaimed the words:
> 'On account of your firm word
> you will live forever, o Dubrovnik! '

Dubrovnik and Vukovar! The Catholic weekly *Voice of the Council* contains a very significant article by Jakov Jukić titled "The Twilight of Two Illusions" in the issue for 24 November 1991. The illusions that Jukić shed was that the policy of anticommunism was principled and that Europe is Christian. We shall not waste any time on the latter illusion, but the first deserves some further comment. Jukić is entirely in the right when he states that Croats thought that the West stood for a great truth, not for mere business and amusement. "It is therefore not surprising," he concludes, "that the people of rich countries experience somebody else's war more as an obstacle to their daily comfort than as a reason for the trying of their conscience. As a result, peace, too, is seen as an equlibrium accomplished by mutual concessions and compromises, rather than a moral effort that is meant to accomplish justice."

The Croats today, more than ever before, stand with the peasant Klasnić from Slavko Kolar's novella: "You know how it is, we are for justice. We believe in justice and we'll not give in." We believe in the epopee of Dubrovnik and Vukovar. Jakov Jukić is right when he says that "every war always and everywhere begins with the discovery of truth about oneself and others. "Today the Vuka and the Danube flow into the blue Adriatic. The novelist Pavao Pavličić, himself from Vukovar, wrote well in his essay on the Danube in November: "It slowly flows in the darkness, and with the rustle of its waters along the underpinned banks, it whispers to the cardplayers that victory and defeat, as everything else, make sense."

(The translation of a speech at the dinner for aid to Vukovar and Dubrovnik, organized by the Society of Alumni of Croatian Universities, Toronto, Ontario, Canada, 6 December 1991)

Luko Paljetak

The City of Measure

Dubrovnik has always been a measured city. It was built with measure, and it established a measure — placing a legal measure in a public place, where it was accessible to everybody, so that anybody could use it to check the measurements, to measure what needed to be measured. *"Our weights forbid cheating or being cheated"* — these are the words inscribed along the rim of the central arch of the Sponza Palace. And another admonition: *"The weight I use to weigh things is the same weight that God uses to weigh me."* The measure of the city and the measure of Man thus became one, in humanity and divineness, in harmony and beauty, which is always a measure — a measure of all measures. Today, Dubrovnik measures inhumanity: the measure of inhumanity with which it has been attacked is the line of division, a perfect line separating humans and non–humans, genuine people and people who are not that.

Historically, Dubrovnik always relied on the power of words rather than the powerful guns, which it had and which themselves were works of art. It relied on the logic of diplomacy, which it skilfully practised, leading the way in this art in Europe and in the world, from whose diplomacy it now awaits mere mercy for its people, its survival and its beauty — the beauty which it thought would be its adequate protection against any barbaric act, especially if it was — as it is — protected by the chivalric shield sporting the colours of UNESCO. Our own Orlando, the knight of our measure, is meanwhile boarded up, as is also Đivo and all the fragile stone porcelain of our palaces, threatened by the tooth of the rhinoceros, the heavy foot of the mastodon, and the trampling of the headless beast.

They have chosen Dubrovnik, the most glorious and least resistant of our cities, and are now destroying it, demonstrating for the umpteenth painful time the horrible power of the person, that, poor man, has no power but the power of brute force. Dubrovnik is at present taking the measure of that force, and will soon be the measure of the fall of that haughty force, for which its message has long been: THE HIGHER THE FLIGHT, THE MORE PAINFUL THE FALL.

Dubrovnik has been built by that same spirit that built the other happy cities of old Europe, which is now deaf to what it hears and blind to what it sees. Dubrovnik is now a heavy weight on its conscience — it is not a Disneyland (whose creator deserves nothing but our grateful praise), but a precious bowl of life on Europe's table, now rudely pushed aside while diplomatic champagne is being sipped leisurely, *méthode charmat*, to the sound of bloodletting in Croatia, *méthode croate*.

Dubrovnik is a city of truth. Truth in a small language is not small truth, but just TRUTH, for which there is no substitute, just as there is none for Dubrovnik. Like Susana, it stands among frenzied old men who seek to compensate for their impotence by parading the erection of their recoilless guns. But all this is to no avail. Dubrovnik is trap. They will not come out of it. Dubrovnik is a phoenix. It would take another Rodin to sculpt the residents of Dubrovnik. All 60,000 of them.

Dubrovnik is the crown of the Croatian cities, and Fort Minčeta is the crown of Dubrovnik, the most glorious fortress on Croatia's checkered coat–of–arms. And it will checkmate the opponent in the castle end–game. For its strength lies not just in the solid rock and stone masonry but also in the powerful spirit of Freedom in which, like the city as a whole, it was built — in the name of human freedom, according to the measure of freedom, which is a measure above all measures. But now the measure has been exceeded, exceeded indeed, gentlemen. *Obliti privatorum!*

Translated by Vladimir Ivir

Luko Paljetak

A DONNA FLORA

Lamento, sopra le spoglie incenerite del parco di
Cannosa nel quale Niko Gučetić Gozze (1581),
affascinato dalla bellezza di Flora Zuzzeri scrisse il suo
DIALOGO DELLA BELLEZZA, DETTO ANTOS

Se sapessi, Flora mia, in che stato è il tuo giardino,
che sterminio, che abbandono! in che fumo e che rovina,
calpestata rosellina! Che amaranto, piede atroce,
quale zoccolo feroce, empio, ha invaso il paradiso
che alla tua beltà fiorì. Se sapessi, Flora mia...

Arde canfora e s'abbrucia, biancospino e anche la canna
che di Pan si fece, a lungo, tanto amabile strumento,
stritolati da una nera, da violenza che li danna:
divorò per sempre il fuoco coi cipressi il mirto e il timo.
Ninfa cara, se sapessi, come ovunque sia tormento.

Si diparte, ora che tutto qui di colpo è reso spento,
con il vano suo tridente, il Nettuno disarmato:
e il suo piede già divora fiamma acerba e dolorosa.
Se sapessi, ninfa mia, come in nulla consumato
si è il sedile al quale, amato... Oh che tempo fu, cortese

di letizia e gentilezza! Che parole ornate, oh Muse,
Niko scelse ad eternare la tua candida bellezza,
a dipingerne il ritratto! Ma ora vedi come il quadro,
Flora Mia, si è già disfatto: in che nero si scompone,
quadro nero di nerume, di un mal nero da morire.

Ma com'è non so, mia ninfa. Muoio e ignoro: a chi funesta
la beltà può mai sembrare? Oggi che triste divaga
il tuo spirito per vuoti, per sentieri desolati:
che su muta pietra piange, lacerato dalla guerra,
il tuo cuore, oh ninfa mia, che una tetra angoscia afferra.

Ma dal pianto, ninfa cara, dalle tue lacrime calde
fiori nuovi fioriranno, Flora mia, e selva fresca:
sì che al folto l'usignolo torni e veda come cresca
nel rigoglio il cinguettare, sì che tornino a sbocciare
salde e forti libertà...

Così tutto sia com'era. Oh sapessi quanto manca
ciò che fu, nel fumo nero: mentre invoco la tua bianca
guancia cui corre il pensiero...

28 ottobre 1991

Traduzione: Frano Čale — Grytzko Mascioni

André Glucksmann

La lumière noire

Les motifs de mon arrivée à Dubrovnik pendant la guerre...

Lorsque j'ai passé mes derniers examens de philosophie, le sujet de la dissertation c'était *Le philosophe dans la cité moderne*. Depuis (et avant), je m'intéresse à la cité moderne parce que je suis philosophe et à la philosophie parce que la cité moderne pose beaucoup de problèmes. D'autre part la guerre pour moi n'est pas quelque chose d'absolument étrange, d'absolument extraordinaire. Je crois que c'est un des problèmes principaux que l'humanité connaît depuis son origine, depuis que l'homme a inventé des haches de pierre et les a enfoncées dans la tête de son voisin. La maîtrise de cette pulsion, de ce phénomène de guerre, c'est la question essentielle et de la civilisation et de la philosophie.

Sur les intellectuels...

A mon avis il y a deux types d'intellectuels, celui qui est prophète de bonheur, qui explique comment il faut vivre, bien vivre, comment l'individu peut acquérir une santé parfaite et comment la collectivité peut entrer au paradis. Je pense que la majorité des intellectuels et des hommes politiques sont des prophètes de bonheur. Et puis il y a des intellectuels qui sont plutôt des prophètes de malheur, c'est–à–dire qui essaient de prévoir ce qui ne va pas afin de l'éviter. Je pense que c'est une minorité, et qu'elle existe depuis les Grecs (Calcas, Tiresias, Cassandra — prophètes de malheur). Dans la Bible il y a aussi beaucoup de prophètes, mais en général ce sont des prophètes qui annoncent les choses qui ne vont pas, les risques, les périls, les malheurs, et ce type de prophètes est minoritaire, mais important. Au 20ème siècle il y a eu beaucoup de prophètes de bonheur, beaucoup trop. Nous avons commis tous les crimes de l'histoire européenne du 20ème siècle au nom du bien, comme le dit Soljenitsyne. C'est pour le bien de la cause que l'on a ouvert des camps de concentration, pour le bien de la race, pour le bien de la classe, pour le bien de la nation, pour le bien de l'humanité, pour le bien de la foi, et il y a eu trop peu de prophètes de malheur. Le plus grand de ces prophètes a été Soljenitsyne qui n'a pas dit qu'il faut aimer tel ou tel Dieu, mais qui a dit qu'il faut regarder le mal en face, qu'il faut regarder le goulag, qu'il faut essayer de comprendre pourquoi il y a eu le goulag et pourquoi nous-mêmes nous avons laissé advenir le goulag et pourquoi nous y avons participé. Soljenitsyne dit: «Je comprends le goulag parce que je regarde en moi-même. Et en moi-même je retrouve le jeune homme que j'étais, qui était un peu stalinien. Donc en moi-même je retrouve les racines du goulag et je comprends le goulag à partir de l'expérience de mes propres pulsions aggressives et autoritaires.» En cela je pense qu'il y a une tradition en Occident, celle de Socrate: connais-toi, toi-même, et celle de Soljenitsyne qui dit finalement la même chose et qui consiste à se confronter à la douleur, à la souffrance, au mal, à la peste, à la peste politique, à la peste sociale, pour essayer de barrer les routes de l'enfer et pour essayer de résister. Donc, l'intellectuel témoin c'est celui, non pas qui prêche le bien, mais qui regarde le mal en face. En cela l'intellectuel témoin n'est pas différent du civil témoin, du simple citoyen témoin.

La guerre en Croatie...

Chaque guerre a ses particularités. Je crois que nous vivons ici une guerre de l'après-communisme. Les Polonais disent que lorsque le communisme s'en va, la société totalitaire s'en retrouve. La société totalitaire a fonctionné comme un frigidaire: elle a gardé toutes les anciennes querelles, toutes les anciennes haines, toutes les anciennes pulsions au frais, elle les a conservées. Mais, disent les Polonais, le frigidaire ne marchait pas tout à fait bien, il y a eu des pannes de courant, et les haines, les pulsions anciennes ont pourri dans le frigidaire, donc sont plus virulentes, plus dangereuses à la sortie qu'à l'entrée du communisme. Et vous remarquerez que la haine entre les Arméniens et les Musulmans, Azeris ou Turcs, c'est la haine de 1915. L'Arménie était integrée à l'Empire soviétique en 1917-1918, et tout est resté dans les haines comme avant. De même entre Roumains et Russes, la querelle entre la Lituanie et l'Empire soviétique, c'est 1940. Il est tout à fait normal de retrouver cette effervescence de haine. Le problème est de savoir comment la régler. Là, je crois que les plus

Pavo Urban / St. Blaise and the shells, December 6, 1991

Pavo Urban / Shelling of the Fort of St. John by guided missiles, November 1991

Milo Kovač / The city walls as a target, November 9–13, 1991

Pavo Urban / Stone dust over the town, December 6, 1991 (his last photo)

Pavo Urban / The first shell on the Old Town, October 23, 1991

Milo Kovač / **The Cathedral immediately after being hit, December 6, 1991**

Milo Kovač / The town in flames, December 6, 1991

Milo Kovač / **Bombing of the port of Gruž, November 1991**

Jadran Kapor (Dubrovački vjesnik) / **Shelling of the mountain Srđ above Dubrovnik, October 1, 1991**

Petar–Marija Radelj / **Shelling of the mountain Srđ, the Crucifix, December 6, 1991**

Pavo Urban / **Parking area behind the Town, November 1991**

Božidar Đukić / **The Old Town port in flames, December 6, 1991**

Pavo Urban / The bleeding car, Montovjerna, November 1991

Milo Kovač / **Shelling of the old port and the Town, November 1991**

Milo Kovač / **The city port in flames, December 6, 1991**

Božidar Đukić / Stradun (the main street of the Old Town) in
flames, December 6, 1991

Božidar Đukić / Stradun (the main street of the Old Town) in flames, December 6, 1991

Božidar Đukić / **Consequences of the shelling of the Old Town (Stradun), December 7, 1991**

Milo Kovač / Shelling and burning of houses on the Stradun —
Placa (Dubrovnik Festival and others), December 6, 1991

Božidar Đukić / Ulica od Puča (a street in the Old Town),
December 6, 1991

Željko Šoletić / **Devastation of a house in the street Široka ulica,
December 6, 1991**

Božidar Đukić / A burnt–out house in the Miho Pracat's street,
December 6, 1991

Matko Biljak / **Destroyed mansion in the Old Town, December 6, 1991**

Božidar Đukić / **Ulica između polača (a street in the Old Town),
December 6, 1991**

profonds et les plus nouveaux ont été les dissidents qui ont été à l'intérieur de l'Empire soviétique. Ce n'est pas le cas de la Yougoslavie qui n'a pas été à l'intérieur de l'Empire soviétique depuis 1948. Là, à l'intérieur de l'Empire soviétique, nous avons l'exemple de gens qui ont pris des précautions devant ce renouvellement de la haine. Dans les annés 70, le cardinal Vishinsky, qui était le primat de Pologne, a declaré aux Allemands: nous les Polonais, nous avons aussi commis des crimes de guerre pendant la 2ème guerre mondiale. Vous savez, tous les Polonais savent que les Allemands en ont commis plus, mais il a désamorcé des haines anciennes en prenant une part de responsabilité dans les événements du passé. Vaclav Havel, lorsq'il a été nommé président, est allé voir les Allemands et a dit publiquement «nous démocrates tchèques, nous avons une responsabilité dans l'expulsion des Sudètes en 1945. C'était un crime historique que la démocratie tchèque a fait avec Stalin. Ça nous a couté très cher parce que cette alliance avec Stalin nous a rendu incapables de résister au stalinisme. Donc, nous nous excusons, nous demandons pardon aux Allemands, et aux Sudètes de les avoir expulsés», et ça a amélioré beaucoup la situation. Je pense que la Croatie avait tout à fait le droit de demander son indépendance, sa liberté, son auto–détermination, au nom d'un nationalisme démocrate. Le problème est que le nationalisme croate a été aussi dans les années 40 fasciste, et que c'est bien évident que les gens d'aujourd'hui ne sont pas les gens d'avant–hier. Mais dans le nationalisme croate, comme dans beaucoup de nationalismes, il y a une tradition mauvaise et une tradition bonne, et il aurait fallu que les responsables Croates disent publiquement qu'ils ont le droit d'être nationalistes. La fierté d'être Croate est tout à fait justifiée, mais qu'elle implique, comprenne en soi toute l'histoire, les bons côtés et les mauvais. Et que donc on se sente responsables, non pas coupables parce que nous n'avons rien fait, mais responsables du passé, et aussi du mauvais passé. Brandt et Kohl sont allés à Auschwitz, Mitterrand et Kohl se sont reconciliés à Verdun, Valensa est allé à Jérusalem.

Enfin, cette façon d'assumer le passé pour désamorcer les haines et pour empêcher leur explosion présente, à mon avis, cette leçon des dissidents, il faudrait, même si c'est un peu tard, qu'elle soit méditée en Croatie.

Le comportement des habitants de Dubrovnik pendant le siège...

Ce que j'ai remarqué à Dubrovnik, c'est que dans une atmosphère de crise, de trouble et de peur, les citoyens de Dubrovnik arrivaient à maîtriser cette peur et cette angoisse sans la cacher. Ils arrivaient à la maîtriser pratiquement en organisant très bien la réception des réfugiés des alentours, la distribution des vivres, la cohabitation dans des conditions absolument pas prévues et très difficiles. Il y a là une volonté morale de vivre normalement dans des circonstances anormales, et de résister à sa propre peur et au désordre mental propagé par l'encerclement, à la pression de cet encerclement. C'est cela que j'ai admiré. Le courage ne consiste pas à tuer ou à détester, ou à haïr l'autre, il consiste d'abord à maîtriser sa propre peur. En cela j'ai trouvé les habitants de Dubrovnik courageux, et je crois que c'est une marque de civilisation et de culture que d'arriver à dominer l'angoisse.

Le problème de sauver Dubrovnik...

Je dirais en paraphrasant Hegel qu'il y a beaucoup de sauveurs, mais qu'à Dubrovnik les gens ne veulent pas de sauveurs. Ils veulent se sauver eux-mêmes. Ils veulent vivre comme ils vivaient avant.

Quand les troupes russes arrivaient dans l'ancienne Allemagne dans les années napoléoniennes, Hegel disait «Il y a beaucoup de libérateurs, mais je ne vois pas de libérés». Je crains que si les troupes serbes envahissaient Dubrovnik, il y aurait beaucoup, beaucoup de libérateurs, mais il n'y aurait personne de libéré. Le problème est assez simple. Sauver les gens de Dubrovnik, c'est leur permettre de vivre comme avant. Il n'y a pas de problèmes, il n'y a pas d'insurrection pro-serbe durement réprimée par les autorités municipales à Dubrovnik, il y a simplement beaucoup de réfugiés, beaucoup de gens dans des hôtels qui vivent dans des conditions extrêmement difficiles, qui ont souvent tout perdu.

La définition de sauver les habitants de Dubrovnik, c'est que les armées se retirent, que l'eau revienne, que la circulation se rétablisse, que les touristes commencent à venir. Il n'y a là aucun problème métaphysique ou idéologique à résoudre.

Hrvoje Kačić

L'humanisme et les humanistes des années 80...

Sous le mot humanisme on a mis beaucoup de choses et n'importe quoi. Il y a eu des gens qui étaient humanistes au début du siècle en pensant que nous étions les meilleurs hommes du monde, nous les Européens éclairés, et que rien de ce qui est humain ne nous est étranger. Cet humanisme optimiste du début du siècle a connu beaucoup de malheurs puisqu'il a deux défauts: d'une part ne pas voir le mal chez les autres et ne pas prévoir l'aggression (par exemple, la France a chanté «tout va très bien Mme la Marquise» quand Hitler était aux portes). C'est le premier défaut: ne pas voir le mal chez les autres. Le deuxième défaut, c'est ne pas voir le mal en soi, en nous–mêmes. Ça a donné les guerres au nom du bien. Ce qui était étonnant n'étaient pas les guerres parce qu'on en a eu toujours, mais des guerres totales, des guerres sans condition, des guerres où on a demandé la reddition complète de l'adversaire. Les grandes guerres, c'est une nouveauté du siècle, elles sont grandes parce qu'elles se font au nom de grandes morales, de grands humanismes, comme les révolutions. Donc, ce danger de l'humanisme, l'Europe l'a durement expérimenté. L'humanisme d'aujourd'hui doit être beaucoup plus tragique et ne doit pas prêcher le bien, mais s'opposer au mal. L'exemple, c'est Soljenitsyne qui ne dit jamais «vous avez eu tort de ne pas croire en mon Dieu et en mon idéal», mais il dit toujours «vous avez eu tort de ne pas regarder le mal en face et de ne pas regarder votre propre participation au mal». Cela veut dire qu'il faut cesser d'applaudir quand on n'est pas d'accord, ensuite il faut essayer de penser par ses propres moyens, parce que chacun est isolé face au mal.

Je dirais que l'humanisme d'aujourd'hui est la solidarité de ceux qui savent qu'au nom du bien on peut tromper, mais que face au mal on peut s'unir. Et cette solidarité est celle que le maître de philosophie de Vaclav Havel, qui s'appelle Patoshcka, définissait comme la solidarité des ébranlés. Nous sommes solidaires parce que nous avons une expérience commune du mal. Un camp de concentration est un camp de concentration, qu'il soit nazi, communiste ou islamique. Une torture policière est une torture policière, qu'elle soit au nom de la Serbie ou au nom de la Croatie. Une dictature est une dictature, peu importe qu'elle soit de gauche ou de droite. La famine est la famine, qu'elle ait lieu en Asie ou en Afrique, qu'elle ait lieu pour les Musulmans ou qu'elle ait lieu pour les catholiques. Il y a des malheurs, des souffrances qui sont planétaires. Et par là il y a un humanisme possible, mondial, qui trouve sa lumière non pas dans le bien, parce qu'il n'y a pas, à ma connaissance, un bien universel, mais qui trouve sa lumière dans le mal, une lumière noire qui éclaire beaucoup.

L'Europe de demain...

Je crois qu'il y a une culture européenne et qu'il y a une Europe en formation, et que cette Europe, évidemment, ne s'arrête pas à Vienne, surtout ne se résume pas aux pensées de la France, aux intelligences française, anglaise et allemande.

La plus grande avancée morale et intellectuelle de la fin du 20ème siècle n'a pas eu lieu en Europe occidentale, mais dans l'ex–Empire soviétique dans le travail, dans la littérature, dans la réflexion et dans la lutte des dissidents (Sakharov, Soljenitsyne). C'est mon premier point, donc, l'Europe englobe tout l'ex–Empire socialiste européen. Deuxième point, la culture européenne est désormais planétaire. On appelle cela la culture occidentale, mais elle est évidemment européenne. Les Américains sont encore très jeunes dans cette culture. La question que pose la culture européenne à la planète est celle de savoir comment s'unir devant les terribles dangers de notre propre puissance. La science ne résout pas le problème moral — elle pose la question morale. La science nous rend capables, en même temps, de nourrir toute la planète et de faire exploser toute la planète — à nous de nous débrouiller.

Pourquoi c'est un problème posé par la culture européenne? Premièrement, parce que la culture européenne a inventé la science et la technique dans leurs formes modernes. Deuxièmement, parce que la culture européenne est la seule culture du monde, de la planète, qui n'ait pas un seul bien, qui n'ait pas une seule conception de l'idéal, qui n'ait pas une seule valeur suprême, qui n'ait pas un seul Dieu. Quand vous vous demandez comment l'Europe sera unie, vous pouvez dire qu'elle ne sera ni tout à fait juive, ni tout à fait catholique, ni tout à fait protestante, ni tout à fait orthodoxe, ni entièrement de gauche (quelle gauche?), ni entièrement de droite (quelle droite?). L'Europe sera pluraliste, elle aura plusieurs valeurs, donc les valeurs de l'Europe sont nécessairement relatives. C'est la seule civilisation qui n'ait pas une valeur suprême, un Dieu suprême, un gouvernement suprême. C'est la seule civilisation qui arrive à être une civilisation sans avoir une seule autorité morale et politique. Ce n'est pas un défaut. C'est une qualité. Car quand on se demande comment la planète sera unie, si vous voulez l'unir sous un seul Dieu, sous une seule religion, est–ce que vous choisissez le Coran, la Bible ou les Evangiles? Donc, la capacité de vivre ensemble sans avoir le même idéal, c'est une capacité tout à fait positive et tout à fait nécessaire au 21ème siècle. C'est pour cela que la planète sera européenne, ou la planète ne sera pas. Et troisièmement, cela ne veut pas dire que tout soit bon dans la culture européenne, cela veut dire simplement que le conflit qu'il y a à l'intérieur de la civilisation européenne devient un conflit planétaire. Et ce conflit existe depuis les Grecs: le conflit entre ceux qui acceptent la démocratie, la libre circulation des biens, des propriétés, des personnes, des idées, des informations, et ceux qui essaient de s'enfermer derrière les murs — les intégristes, disons, qui essaient de créer une société close pour se défendre contre l'influence de la libre circulation des hommes et des idées, le tout pour ne pas être déracinés. Cette opposition–là existait déjà en Grèce. La tentation de s'enfermer derrière les murs fut déjà au centre de la tragédie grecque. Platon dit: «Une ville qui s'enferme, c'est une ville qui pourrit.» Cette opposition gouverne, à mon avis, notre définition du 21ème siècle, de la planète et de l'Europe — ou bien nous acceptons la libre circulation des hommes, des idées, des richesses, ce qui s'appelle la démocratie européenne, ou bien nous la refusons, et ça s'appelle, alors, l'intégrisme qui est aussi européen. Les murs ont été construits dans la culture européenne. Le mur de l'Atlantique a été construit par les Allemands, le mur de Berlin par les Russes, et le voile islamique n'est pas un exotisme — c'est aussi une réaction intégriste qui appartient à notre culture. Les Iraniens, les Shiites iraniens, ce sont des néo–platoniciens, ce ne sont pas des sauvages qui ne font pas partie de notre culture.

La culture européenne est partagée. Elle a une tendance à l'intégrisme, et elle a une tendance aux lumières et à la démocratie. Et c'est cette bataille qui est la bataille fondamentale de tout le 20ème siècle. On a détruit un certain nombre d'intégrismes (l'intégrisme hitlérien, l'intégrisme stalinien), mais il en reste pas mal qui peuvent s'appuyer soit sur le nationalisme, soit sur la religion, et puis sur les pulsions d'égoïsme, d'avidité et aussi de peur et d'angoisse, qui existent dans toutes les populations.

Extraits de l'entretien, Dubrovnik, le 3 décembre 1991.

Préparé par Vesna Čučić

Jean D'Ormesson

Une petite tache sur l'Europe

Les motifs de mon arrivée à Dubrovnik pendant la guerre...

J'ai été très heureux à Dubrovnik dans des moments de paix. Je me souviens que j'avais passé ici des journées que je n'ai pas oubliées. Il m'a semblé que c'était difficile de continuer à rire et à m'amuser quand des gens que j'avais connus ici étaient dans la souffrance et dans la guerre. Et c'est ce qui m'a décidé à lancer le premier appel en faveur de Dubrovnik dans la presse. En ce moment-là je ne savais pas très bien ce qu'il fallait faire. Je pensais simplement qu'il fallait attirer l'attention du monde sur le sort de Dubrovnik. A l'égard de Dubrovnik il y avait deux attitudes possibles: la première qui avait été prise par beaucoup, par les Nations Unies, par l'UNESCO, par l'Europe, c'était de ne rien faire du tout. Et la deuxième, que j'avais moi-même envisagée, c'était qu'un certain nombre de gouvernements devraient prendre des mesures violentes, je n'aurais pas été tout à fait hostile à l'envoie d'un ou deux bateaux de guerre devant Dubrovnik. Et puis je me suis aperçu qu'il y avait une troisième voie qui était celle des humanitaires. Cette voie consistait à apporter une aide aux femmes, aux enfants et à utiliser la méthode de la présence. C'est à dire, selon la formule de Glucksmann qui est très belle, d'encercler par l'opinion publique ceux qui encerclaient Dubrovnik. Dans le monde moderne la communication est devenue si forte qu'il est possible de faire reculer la guerre par des moyens qui n'appartiennent plus à la guerre mais qui appartiennent à la paix. En ce sens il y avait une action possible et c'est pour cette raison que je suis là. J'avais même dit que je viendrais par tous les moyens possibles et que si la ville était encerclée je me ferais parachuter.

Sur l'engagement de la France à Dubrovnik...

La France a historiquement une amitié avec les Serbes. Il y a les souvenirs de la Première guerre mondiale. J'ai moi–même un grand–père qui a été ambassadeur en Serbie. Il y a un livre qui a paru en serbe sur les mémoires de ce grand–père et de sa mission en Serbie. Moi–même j'ai écrit un article qui s'appelle *La Serbie que nous aimons*. Mais la Serbie que nous aimons c'est une Serbie pacifique, une Serbie démocratique, une Serbie qui respecte les droits de l'homme, et je crois qu'il y a en ce moment à Belgrade des mouvements de cet ordre et des mouvements qui sont dirigés contre le gouvernement de M. Milošević.

Je dois dire qu'au départ je pense que les Français, devant le conflit entre les Serbes et les Croates, n'avaient pas une idée très arrêtée. Ils considéraient la chose avec équilibre. Et petit à petit, avec les nouvelles qui nous sont parvenues, la balance a penché en faveur des Croates. Et les Français ont été obligés de revoir leur attitude à l'égard des Serbes parce que les attaques sur Vukovar, les attaques sur Osijek et, peut–être surtout, les attaques sur Dubrovnik (parce que Dubrovnik est plus connu chez nous, parce que Dubrovnik est protégé en un sens par sa beauté, par ses monuments, et peut–être en effet que ce n'est pas juste, je pense qu'on a souffert encore plus à Vukovar et à Osijek qu'à Dubrovnik) en tout cas toutes ces attaques qui sont, naturellement, contraires aux droits des hommes, ont fait pencher la balance en faveur des Croates. Je prends ici, évidemment, une position politique que peut–être les humanitaires ne prennent pas. On ne peut pas dans la guerre actuelle dire «Voilà, il y a d'un côté les Croates et de l'autre les Serbes, nous ne nous occupons pas de savoir qui a raison, nous apportons simplement notre aide à ceux qui sont malheureux». On pourrait trouver aussi du côté croate des injustices, des abus, des violences, naturellement. J'en suis sûr qu'on peut trouver aussi du côté des Serbes des vertus et des qualités. Mais dans la guerre, dans cette guerre il y a tout de même un côté qui est l'assaillant et l'autre côté qui est la victime. Et bien je suis du côté des victimes.

La propagande serbe et la Croatie...

La propagande serbe est dirigée sur le fait que les Croates sont des fascistes et que pendant la guerre les fascistes ont regné en Croatie. Ma réponse est assez simple: il y a eu des fascistes en Allemagne, nous collaborons aujourd'hui avec des Allemands parce que les Allemands ont subi un fascisme et que maintenant l'Allemagne est devenu un pays démocratique; il y a eu des fascistes en France, il a y eu des fascistes partout, comme il y a eu des communistes partout. J'essaye de me tenir à égale distance des fascistes et des communistes. J'ai le sentiment qu'aujourd'hui le vrai danger est du côté de la survivance de l'armée rouge du côté serbe. Il n'y a plus d'armée rouge dans aucun pays qui était l'Europe de l'Est. L'armée rouge existe encore en URSS, mais le pouvoir civil la contrôle et la combat. L'armée fédérale est tout de même une sorte de reliquat de l'armée rouge et on peut considérer que le régime serbe est de quelque façon un régime qui est passé du marxisme au nationalisme, à un nationalisme agressif et il n'est pas tout à fait interdit de considérer le régime serbe comme une sorte de national communisme. Le fascisme croate appartient au passé et le national communisme serbe est toujours présent.

Le comportement des habitants de Dubrovnik pendant le siège...

Je suis porté à croire que quand une ville comme Dubrovnik est assiégée par quelqu'un, la responsabilité est d'abord sur celui qui assiège. Il est difficile de faire passer pour victime celui qui assiège les autres. Il me semble qu'ici il y a une généalogie de la haine. Elle vient plutôt de celui qui assiège. Maintenant que celui qui est assiégé se met ensuite à haïr celui qui assiège, mon Dieu, même si ça existe on peut peut–être le comprendre.

Dans la position serbe, sa propagande, sa pression, un des points qui revient souvent et qui m'a été dit c'est que Dubrovnik n'est pas une ville croate. Je ne suis pas spécialiste de ce domaine, mais j'ai tout de même le sentiment que les habitants de Dubrovnik ne sont pas Serbes. Alors, est–ce qu'ils sont Croates ou est–ce qu'ils ne sont pas Croates, je ne le sais pas non plus, mais l'unanimité des gens qui ont envie de leur indépendance me paraît d'une évidence tout à fait claire.

Le problème de sauver Dubrovnik...

Je suis persuadé que maintenant tout le monde en France a été frappé de l'unanimité croate et on sait que Dubrovnik veut rester croate. Et on sait aussi que l'armée fédérale est très puissante et qu'il est possible que sur le terrain l'armée fédérale ait remporté des succès. Mais moralement, je crois que c'est la cause croate qui a gagné, que la guerre psychologique et morale a été gagnée par les Croates.

D'abord j'ai été attaqué en France même, par les Français qui m'ont dit «vous voulez sauver Dubrovnik parce que vous voulez sauver les pierres et vous ne penser pas aux hommes». Bien sûr que je pense aux hommes, la vie d'un homme, d'une femme, d'un enfant est supérieure à un tableau, à une colonne, à une corniche quelque belle qu'elle soit. Dubrovnik fait partie, c'est l'UNESCO qui l'a dit, du patrimoine culturel de l'humanité.

Il faut sauver la ville et il faut sauver en même temps les hommes et les femmes qui sont dans la ville. Il faut que la ville ne soit pas détruite. Mais l'armée fédérale peut dire aussi «il ne faut pas détruire la ville, rendez vos armes, rendez vous, et nous garantissons que la ville ne sera pas détruite». Alors, il y a aussi quelque chose qui est la volonté nationale, la volonté d'indépendance, l'honneur de ce qu'ils sont, et je comprends très bien que cette solution ne sera pas acceptée par les gens de Dubrovnik. Et on ne peut que respecter les gens de Dubrovnik parce qu'ils ne veulent pas se rendre à ces conditions. Après tout, il faut admirer plus les gens qui résistent que les gens qui ne résistent pas. Pétain aussi disait «Il faut sauver le pays et il ne faut pas résister.» C'était de Gaulle qui avait dit «Il faut sauver le pays, mais il faut résister.» Eh bien, je crois qu'il faut sauver les pierres et qu'il faut sauver en même temps les gens.

Si on avait envoyé, la France, l'Angleterre, l'Allemagne (je sais bien qu' elle n'a pas le droit parce qu'il y a un traité), mais enfin si les Etats Unis, la France, l'Angleterre et quelques autres pays avaient envoyé les bateaux de guerre sur la côte, ça ne m'aurait pas fait de peine, je n' aurais pas poussé les grands cris. Je me demande même s'il ne fallait pas le faire.

Enfin, je comprends qu'un gouvernement puisse hésiter, mais alors on ne peut pas faire moins que ce que nous faisons et que c'est le minimum de ce que nous pouvons faire: d'avoir une présence ici, de faire comprendre à ceux qui encerclent la ville que le monde est solidaire de ceux qu'ils assiègent, qu'ils ne peuvent pas y pénétrer sans que le monde entier se soulève contre eux et sans les plus grands risques.

On peut penser que Dubrovnik mène une bataille d'arrière-garde, c' est-à-dire qu'il défend des positions qui appartiennent au passé, comme une armée qui recule devant une histoire qui avance. Eh bien, je ne crois pas du tout. Je crois, au contraire, que sa bataille est celle de l'avenir et que ce qui appartient au passé c'est l'armée rouge. La liberté, l'indépendance nationale, les droits de l'homme, la démocratie, voilà ce qui est l'avenir. On ne peut pas imposer à des gens ce qu'ils ne veulent pas. Si vous les Croates vous vouliez prendre Belgrade je serais contre vous.

Alors, vous allez avoir un problème, c'est le problème des minorités serbes. Il faudra, naturellement, que les Croates protègent ou trouvent un moyen de vivre avec les minorités serbes. La façon dont les Serbes se conduisent avec les Croates n'est pas un modèle pour la façon dont les Croates doivent se conduire avec les Serbes.

L'attitude de l'Europe à l'égard de Dubrovnik...

Je trouve que l'Europe s'est extraordinairement mal conduite dans cette affaire. Je trouve que le gouvernement français aurait pu faire mieux et plus, mais enfin il y a Kouchner. Je ne suis pas de même partie que le gouvernement auquel appartient Kouchner, mais je trouve que Kouchner a fait beaucoup. Je trouve que l'Europe aurait dû et pu faire plus et, qu'au moment où l'Europe va se constituer, le nom de Dubrovnik, qui aurait pu être quelque chose qui donne un sens, un éclat, un élan à l'Europe, est quelque chose, au contraire, qui va être comme une petite tache sur l'Europe. Si jamais il arrivait malheur à Dubrovnik, alors là ça ne serait pas une tache, ça serait une catastrophe pour l'Europe et l'Europe ne se ferait pas s'il arrivait malheur à Dubrovnik. Mais même si (ce que je souhaite et ce que je crois) Dubrovnik est sauvé, ce n'est pas quelque chose de glorieux pour l'Europe, c'est quelque chose de glorieux pour ces gens de Dubrovnik qui ont résisté.

Extraits de l'entretien du 3 décembre 1991 à Dubrovnik

Préparé par Vesna Čučić

Hrvoje Kačić

Dubrovnik and the Calamities of War

We are greatly indebted to Dom. Marin. He, through Pomet*, sent a message to the world that "war is the bane/calamity of human nature". Generations in Dubrovnik grew up understanding the radi-ance of this remark — even at a time when their compatriots from other regions of Croatia were caught up in the storms of war: even outside the borders of their homeland, often against their will; and too frequently in the service of foreigners.

But the experiences, and the teaching, of our ancestors have not managed to help us preserve from the horrors of war this "Croatian Athens", this gentle "Dubrava" (oakwood) of the Croatian south. Such horrors are alien to the heritage of European sensibility, at least at the end of the second millennium.

Perhaps the example of the Second World War contributed to our hopes, our expectations, that Dubrovnik might have missed the tears, human sacrifices and victims, bombardments, the destruction or dev-astation of whole regions. We believed that we could have threaded our way peacefully through the Scylla of the decadence of communism and the Charybdis of the "second Yugoslavia" which had been built on communist ideology. For we had been educated in the values of Dub-rovnik: Dubrovnik, which had been recognised not only in Europe but throughout the wider world as a pearl of civilization, a jewel of archi-tecture, the unification of the harmony of nature; and an Athens of the spirit, of culture, civilization, traditional values, tolerance, openness, and mutuality. Thus we were secure in the belief that Serbian extrem-ism and chauvinism could not subdue us.

How wrong we were. We underestimated the nature and structure of the so–called Yugoslav army. For even when that sad army — which had been neither "national" nor "Yugoslav" since January 24 1991

---

*   Marin Držić (1508–1568) is the most famous writer of the Croatian Renaissance, and among the first Croatian playwrights. *Pomet* is leading person in Držić's comedy "Uncle Maroje".

when it put off its mask — clearly and publicly threatened to remain the main political force in ex–Yugoslavia; even then, it was still believed that this army would not make organized strides into crimes of the dimensions which it was later to commit.

It was well known that the army had resources of enormous and deadly power; but unfortunately we underestimated a fact which had already been adequately verified and is, for that army, an annihilating scar: the extent to which it is prepared to destroy for the sake of destruction itself, to shoot just to kill and to wound, to capture for the prizes of plunder, and is willing to accept the role of an occupying force.

Now, as we think of the calamities of war and of Dubrovnik, and of those dinosaurs in their olive–gray generals' uniforms as well as other human relics with the same uniforms and equipped with weapons from those same arsenals, we can say (it is not an excuse, but an explanation) that we were mistaken: mistaken about the nature of the monster that was threatening us. History will later pronounce on whether this mistake was excusable.

One of the leading partisan generals, Peko Dapčević, addressed an appeal to the Allied Airforce Headquarters in Italy, back at the beginnig of 1944. He requested that the bombers of the allies' squadrons, as they made their way to operate against targets in Hungary and Romania (Ploesti), should not overfly Dubrovnik; because it would be so harmful if there were an accident and an aeroplane crashed on the town with its dangerous load — damage to Dubrovnik would mean such a great loss to European culture. We were duped by this memory, assuming that the army, boasting loyalty to its partisan roots, had kept something of Dapčević's spirit; and that through its military academies, its specializations, and its services in foreign countries it would have developed a code of military behaviour that prohibited it from permitting itself the brutality that characterises aggressors, conquerors, and occupiers.

It is obvious that we were wrong. But before we try to describe how and why we were wrong, and since we have just mentioned partisans in connection with Dubrovnik, we want to ensure that nobody is mistaken in one regard. That is: the calvary of Dubrovnik began with the arrival of partisans in the region in October 1944. It began then, because in that first post–war period the "liberators" forced upon the Croats of Dubrovnik and its surroundings a horrible tribute, paid in blood. In scarcely any village or hamlet did the wives and mothers not go into mourning. In the town itself more than ten priests and monks were executed, as were hundreds upon hundreds of ordinary citizens and residents of the Dubrovnik region.

In the interests of truth I should note that Vladimir Dedijer — when I met him accidentally in spring 1971 at a cocktail party in the Yugoslav Embassy in Washington — told me (in the presence of an honest partisan general, Danilo Trampuz): "We were unjust to Dubrovnik, when thinking–back to the partisans and the so–called National Liberation Army". Someone was curious and asked: "Why?" His answer was very direct: "We let a lot of people get killed there", and he continued: "Tito sent me to Dubrovnik at the end of 1944 to stop the executions, but by then it was already too late".

Dubrovnik was the first such episode; and thinking of Srijem, Bačka, Tovarnik, and other towns and places throughout Croatia, testimonies such as Dedijer's corroborate the fact that even people such as he were entrusted to seek alibis for all the horrors that took place in the post–war reality. Executions became less frequent in the ensuing months. Everything about the selection of atrocities and the decision whether to announce them to the people or conceal them (if indeed there were any system in the selection, or any criteria for decision) leads us to conclude that none of these crimes had the function of revenge or punishment; rather they were to frighten, to conquer, to uproot dreams of democracy and freedom.

"Quod ab initio vitiosum est tractu tempore convalescere non potest" ("what was a crime from the start cannot be mitigated by the passage of time").

In the numerous criminal proceedings concerning bolshevist savagery, proceedings which, of necessity, continued long after the Resolution of the Informbureau, many citizens of Dubrovnik lost their youth and manhood in the prisons and camps of Lepoglava, Stara Gradiška, Zenica, etc.

So too now, just at a time when we were hoping that the winds from Europe with her established democracies would uproot the causes of armed hostility, our "Dubrava", unhappily, followed the destinies of many other Croatian towns and villages, became a victim of the storms of war.

The transition–period from totalitarian communism into democracy does not reveal a simple development; especially not when it is contemporaneous with the rotting of the worn–out model of multinational state–communities, as they squirm and tumble in insoluble economic chaos because of their enslavement by an ideological utopia.

Throughout the whole first half of 1991, all relevant international opinion — some reluctantly, some not — followed–along with Bush's determination to preserve the strategy of retaining the status quo. In this they were influenced by the potential for drama in the ex–USSR, and the tragedy of the war in ex–Yugoslavia. Soon after that Roland Dumas, then both French Minister of Foreign Affairs and President of the Security Council of the United Nations, said nostalgically (when referring to circumstances in the USSR and the SFRY) before a world–wide audience that we were witnesses to the crumbling of the last two colonial empires of Europe.

To understand better the various directions taken by the final episode in the dissolution of those two artificial creations — both set up in a whirlpool of chaos, violence, war, cruelty, and socialist revolution — it is essential to stress certain differences between them. These can be seen right now, as this last act in the life–tragedies of millions of people takes place. This last act represents the end of the world for some. But simultaneously, for innumerable numbers of people and even for whole nations, it represents the dawning of the day of long–sought freedom and democracy.

In the Soviet Union a radical cleansing, and the first phase of transformation, is taking place in a relatively quiet way. But in Yugoslavia that same process is degenerating into a state of undeclared war. The reasons for this bifurcation can be inferred from the following:

(a) In ex–Yugoslavia communism was either defeated or collapsed in Slovenia first, then in Croatia, then in Macedonia and in Bosnia–Herzegovina. This took place away from the state's centre of power, Belgrade; there communism continued its tyranny under a different name. By contrast, communism in the USSR collapsed in the power–centre itself, in Moscow, in the Russian Federation. (I believe that the events in the Baltic Republics, even though they occurred before those in Moscow, are relatively marginal; this because of the hugely disproportionate significance of events in Russia when we take into account all the relevant factors.) Thus, with the collapse of communism in Moscow itself, the military machine was left disorientated; despite the efforts of some of the generals, it was not engaged as a political arbitrator. In Yugoslavia on the other hand the communist defeat in Slovenia and Croatia brought about a blending of objectives between the Serbian oligarchic communist authorities and the Yugoslav — or rather, Serbian — army, an army raised in and poisoned by communism; an army that ignored the organs of federal government.

(b) Serbia, which many of its citizens assumed to be synonymous with Yugoslavia, or if not that at least as the dominant federal unit is becoming an unattractive continental Balkan mini–state with all its uncertainties and burdens, especially the mammoth army (because of its geopolitical situation, natural resources, working habits, size, population, resources, economic potential etc.). But Russia is still definitely a world superpower, from the Baltic and Black seas to the Pacific.

(c) In a critical historical period Gorbachev and Yeltsin happened to be in control, as leaders of the Soviet Union and Russia respectively. Both ex–communists; but as rational and realistic politicians they understood the demands of the time and opted for dialogue, negotiation, compromise, and peaceful solutions. By contrast and most unfortunately the leaders of Yugoslavia (actually Serbia) at that crucial moment were Jović, Milošević, Kadijević, and Adžić; aggressive totalitarians who wanted to keep Serboslavia under the name of Yugoslavia, resorting to compulsion and even war and bloodshed.

(d) Thanks to the common sense of responsible people, Russia has become a permanent member of the Security Council of the United Nations; and is allowing access, where the needs are unavoidable, to international support–structures, financial and otherwise. Serbia on the contrary under its neocommunist leadership (with Montenegro it is the only residue of European communism), using the former federal army to implement its repressive policies — first in Kosovo, then in Slovenia, later in Croatia, now and in the future in Herzeg–Bosnia — remains deaf to every appeal and resolution which emerge from the policies of the world community and particularly the European community. It is sinking into isolation. Pigheadedly, it is exposing itself to sanctions; these will become ever more strict and effective until Serbia undergoes its own metamorphosis, and thus matures into a partner of nations, in conformity with the standards required by the international community.

Colonialism and democracy are eliminating each other. Despotism cannot be improved; only destroyed.

In such historic circumstances, members of the present generations of all non–Serbian nations inside the borders of former Yugoslavia have been confronted by the struggle for survival of their own nation. We are witnessing that painful process, within which the victims, and the losses, are not equally distributed.

In parallel with this process in ex–Yugoslavia, Europe and the USA especially (the USSR is engaged fully with its own turbulence) have been preoccupied with the war in the Gulf. Yugoslavia is sinking into the darkness of war. The USA, surprised, unprepared, and confused, left the initiative to Europe; only recently has it undertaken more direct action with respect to Bosnia and Herzegovina, as it came to understand that although there is blood knee–deep in exhausted Croatia, worse is to come in Herzeg–Bosnia. Up until that time it fell back only upon resolutions and statements, always stressing that the USA will accept no solution that has not been reached by peaceful means — which, in the language of the Balkan Bolshevists, Byzantines, and barbarians, means that force can be used in order to destroy any chance either for an evolution, or a solution. Whereas Europe, with its collective decision–making system and a rotating six–monthly presidency plods always *after* the events.

As the dinosauric generals and paranoid Milošević just go on, the sirens of death and destruction sing a requiem for Yugoslavia, that common state of the southern Slavs which will be remembered as a Yugo–tragedy. According to its Constitution of 1974, Yugoslavia already had in place two important elements required for a confederation; parity and consensus. But these were not respected in any important matters, because everything and everyone were governed by the only orthodoxy, the communist party, until it was squeezed out by the beginnings of democracy.

Once all the efforts made by Slovenians and Croats to transform the common state into a genuine confederation received no response, the results of the Slovenian plebiscite and the Croatian referendum were foregone conclusions. Only the speed of their implementation could have been changed.

Clearly, the only option that remained was the declaration of independence and self–reliance with which Dubrovnik approached its own crucifixion as an integral part of Croatia whose sons, between Dravograd and Serbia, had had a similar experience at one moment of history, in 1945.

Aggressive conquerors are trying to realise Serbia's long–standing aspiration and presumptuous ambition: to gain an exit to the sea.

For, on October 1st, with no reason but with a clear aim, they launched their attack on Dubrovnik. They are not fully satisfied with the sea owned by their southern satellite. They want their own exit to the sea; not just for economic reasons but for their vanity, violence, arrogance, and for the sake of further plunder.

Consider the timing of this attack. The heroism of Vukovar and its citizens had had a certain influence on public opinion in Belgrade, and in Serbia in general. For too long, in fact for days and weeks, the Bel-

Miljenko Mojaš / Damaged cupola of the bell–tower of the
Franciscan church (damaged Museum Rupe in the background),
December 6, and October 23, 1991

Milo Kovač / **House in flames in the Ulica od Puča near St. Joseph's Church, December 6, 1991**

Milo Kovač / **Franciscan Monastery (Minorites), December 6, 1991.**

Božidar Đukić / Shelling of the Library of the Franciscan
Monastery by guided missiles, December 6, 1991

Damir Fabijanić / Church Sigurata, Old Town, June 1992

Božidar Đukić / Damaged balustrade and façade of the of St. Blaise's church, December 6, 1991

Božidar Đukić / **Damaged Great Onofrio's Fountain, December 6, 1991**

Božidar Đukić / **Shelling of the Old Town nucleus (from what is left of the burnt–out top of the Hotel »Imperial«), December 6, 1991**

Milo Kovač / Witnesses — destroyed mansion in the Old Town,
December 6, 1991

Božidar Đukić / **Aftermath of the shelling of the Old Town,
December 6, 1991.**

Željko Šoletić / **The fountain on the Gundulić's square, attacked, May 29 and June 20, 1992**

Damir Fabijanić / **Baroque staircase, next the Jesuit church, June 1992**

Željko Šoletić / **Balustrade on the bridge leading to the Old Town, June 3, 1992**

Željko Šoletić / **The Residence Skočibuha — the Scientific Library,
June 8, 1992**

Ana Opalić / Damaged façade of a house on the Stradun,
December 6, 1991

Željko Šoletić / After the destruction in the street Široka ulica,
December 7, 1991

Milo Kovač / Damaged city walls, December 6, 1991

Željko Šoletić / **Church Sigurata, Old Town, May 31, 1992**

Željko Šoletić / **Stained–glass window in the Sacristy of the Franciscan Monastery, June 8, 1992**

Željko Šoletić / **Franciscan church hit by a shell, June 1992**

Milo Kovač / **The damaged balustrade of St. Blaise's church, December 6, 1991**

Milo Kovač / **Dubrovnik roofs and fortress Minčeta, December 6, 1991**

Milo Kovač / Dead pigeon on the Luža square, December 6, 1991

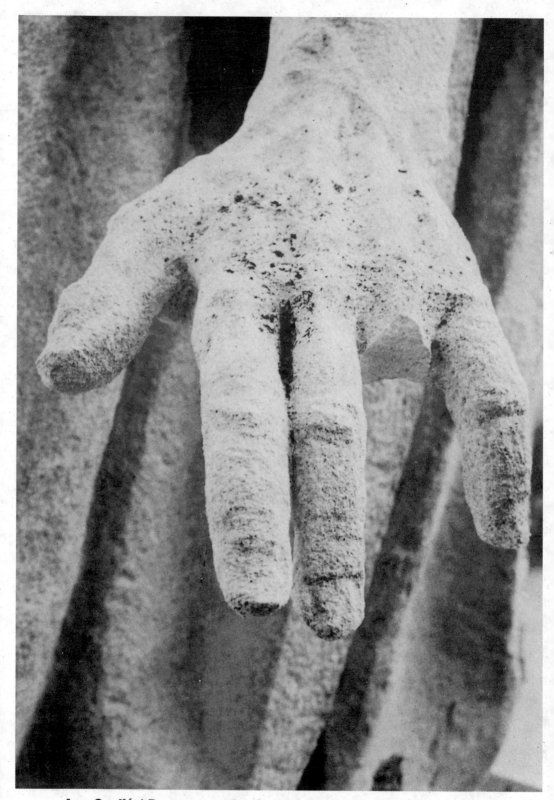

Ana Opalić / Damage on the Cathedral, detail, December 6, 1991

Željko Šoletić / **Damaged Statue of St. Blaise on the Cathedral,
June 8, 1992**

Željko Šoletić / **Monastery of St. Clara, May 29 and June 8, 1992**

Željko Šoletić / **The city bell–tower, June 8, 1992**

Željko Šoletić / New holes in the roofs of Dubrovnik, June 18, 1992

grade media had been feeding the public with the story that any day Vukovar would surrender and be "freed". So day after day the agit–prop "Goebbelses" had to paint over their false forecasts and lies. Impatient appetites had to be assuaged by another gift; and that role was assigned to Dubrovnik. Dubrovnik was thus an indirect victim of heroic Vukovar. But in Vukovar Serbian militants lost their striking power; in Dubrovnik Serbia lost its face.

The conference in the Hague started at the beginning of September 1991. Belgrade figured out that this was the last, and for that reason the best, moment for plunder. Even before the Serbian and Montenegran representatives had reached the Hague, the USA and the European Community had already laid down a clear and indisputable condition: there was to be no changing of borders by force. But perfidious Serbia played a wrong, but under the circumstances the sole remaining, card — the so–called "self–determination of the nation". If this was so valuable in the eyes of the USA and Croatia, why couldn't it be so concerning pieces of Croatia; especially Dubrovnik, which was the most valuable region for Serbia. An antibureaucratic revolution; autonomy; a free republic. Serbia was trying to tempt Dubrovnik with the offer that under Serbia's protection it could "enjoy" itself like Monaco.

At that moment Croatia was passing through its crucifixion. Eastern Slavonia was being attacked from all sides; the line Okućani–Lipik–Virovitica, and then Lika, the traffic–route of Karlovac–Rijeka, are bombarded; the Maslinica bridge is demolished, followed by the Obrovac–Benkovac line towards Zadar and Šibenik; threats come from Peruča (the hydro–electric power station) and the carcinogenic foci which are the barracks throughout the "remaining remains" of Croatia; Ploče is under assault from the sea. In the minds of the generals, Neum is one of the remnants of Yugoslavia. In August 1991 mobs of plunderers were mobilized, no matter whether they were army reservists or any other kind of "bearded band of brigands" (as the so–called JNA was described by Douglas Hurd, the British Minister for Foreing Affairs, in August 1991); mobilized with the warcries: "prepare yourselves, prepare" for plunder and theft.

Far from the rest of the exhausted regions of Croatia's indivisible corpus, its southern part was supposed, in the military–strategic plans devised by generals with their blacked–out minds and their raging warriors, to be an easy catch. They expected just to walk into the town, find some marionettes — with beards or without — and enrich Serbia with a seventh autonomous republic. During these storms of war, Dub-

49

rovnik has lost everything except the people and the wonderful youth prepared to defend their native soil with their own lives.

Military forces invade the territory from the east, from Boka. Slano, to the west, is being destroyed; and the hinterland is under attack from Trebinje. Brgat is putting up tough resistance even though the enemy is absolutely dominant in both air and sea. The dragons of the air are demolishing Croatia's sacred objects inside Dubrovnik, and the dragons of the sea are destroying the ports, cultural monuments, civilian property, churches, and hotels; while, as a gift from the liberators, they throw explosives into museums and palaces even through the windows of the city walls and fortresses.

Geographically separated from its homeland, Dubrovnik with extreme effort is finding the power to defend itself. Young men from the villages, from cafes, from their places of work, from their schools and faculties, are taking up arms. Small fast boats find their way by night between gunboats and cliffs. Young men arrive from the sea; students leave their universities, friends from Korčula, Split, Solin, Opuzen, Zagreb, Vukovar, Herzegovina are joining them. At the very last moment military experts are arriving from Benkovac, Slavonija, Sinj, Omiš and Lastovo. By night and day so–called "televisions" (a form of Molotov cocktail) are being made in people's homes: the only weapons not in short supply. The very same Serbian army is donating to Croatia professional officers — those too honourable and decent to serve the evil under the five–pronged red star, together with the četnik symbols, which had gone so far along their criminal path. Military staff are being recruited; the sea blockade broken through.

Despite all the resources Croatia can raise, Dubrovnik is becoming a new Guernica and Srđ a new Alcasar. This symbiosis of Alcasar attacked and destroyed by "those on the left", and Guernica demolished by "those on the right" — is a fascinating parallel for Dubrovnik and Srđ, because what has befallen Dubrovnik and Croatia during this war comes from a widely–representative spectrum: ranging from the Balkans' most extreme fascist right to the bolshevists' most extreme left... catching–up anyone willing to plunder, steal, and rob. The evidence is everywhere to be seen.

Contrary to the achievements of contemporary Europe, under Milošević's sway various Adžićes have been homogenized shoulder–to–shoulder. In the summer of 1991 Adžić ordered his newly–promoted officers to "use all their knowledge and skill to achieve the objectives of the October Revolution": and various Arkans and Hadžićes have been pulled together as well. The fetters are Šešelj's, Bora Jović's, and

B. Kostić's. So the far left and the far right have united to create force, violence and war, and to generate the hatred that was promulgated in the "Memorandum" of the Serbian Academy of Arts and Sciences. It is a familiar fact that hatred is the most dangerous of explosives.

This is the first war that will go down in world history as an ideological one that has been invented, worked–out, and directed under the auspices of an "Academy". ˙

With the examples of Dubrovnik and Vukovar, cities of heroes in the far east of the Croatian south and the far east of the north, Serbia has shown and proved that it can destroy but cannot build.

The schemer's illusions and traps are often easily recognizable by the slogans launched from Belgrade. To give a few examples: Vuk Karadžić's "Serbs, all and everywhere": Pera Živković's when monarchist dictatorship came in, "Unity–fraternity": this was paraphrased by Josip Broz as "Fraternity–unity" when he installed his bolshevist dictatorship, but the inversion of the words does not change the essence of the thing. Then we have the generals' "Movement for Yugoslavia", "Better a grave than a Euro–slave": Milošević's "All Serbs in one state" — which means that "Nobody is allowed to beat you", but does not mean that "those same ones are banned from killing": Paroški's "You have the right to kill everyone, as one might kill a dog outside the fence" (this was said in Jagodnjak–Baranja, while Croatia still had de facto power there); or Šešelj's in the Serbian parliament, "All Croats must be expelled from Serbia".

It is difficult to imagine Šešelj renouncing his favourite thesis "Karlobag–Ogulin–Karlovac–Virovitica", to which he added that "Rijeka is the largest Serbian port".

It is quite superfluous to comment in any way upon the shock–value and the threat of the messages in such slogans as these.

One must believe that it is a fundamental right of every person to evolve in his mentality, views, beliefs, ethics, and morality: but we fear that often this cannot happen without the catharsis of trauma and shock. Through this catharsis even primitive people, fed from Belgrade, will have to pass; as well as, unfortunately, not a few Belgrade academics as well. The process will be slow, but it is unavoidable.

The truth about Dubrovnik, and not only about Dubrovnik but specifically about the experience of the people of Dubrovnik; the truth about the dead and displaced; about the dimensions of suffering; about the extent of destruction and thoroughness of devastation: about the volume of plunder; about the unsung examples of courage of the killed and of survivors; about the tragic death of the author Milan Milišić (a Serb by birth but a Dubrovniker by education, a member of the Croatian Authors' Society), killed on his doorstep during one of the first October bombardments of Dubrovnik — these truths will probably contribute to speeding–up this unavoidable process of catharsis. Finally there is the truth about the number, disposition, pride, and honour of the many Serbs who remained in Dubrovnik along with the rest of their fellow–citizens. All of these collectively fretted and suffered, forged their strength, built up their obstinacy, strengthened their resistance, helped each other, counted the days until the siege would end, cursed their attackers, conquerors, and plunderers, and waited for the moment when the gang would withdraw or be expelled from the area of Dubrovnik and from the whole of Croatia.

What could be recommended is the organization of a photo–documentary exhibition, along with existing video footage, about the destruction of Dubrovnik (especially its old historical nucleus) and its surroundings; and to display it in Belgrade and Podgorica to familiarize the public their with the acts and crimes committed. It is important that they should know that during the offensive against the fortress Imperial on Srđ, which was undertaken by "special forces" from Niš on St. Nicholas' Day 1991, there was among the numerous heroic defenders a very effective contribution from one man. He was a Dubrovnik athlete and a Serbe, for whom Croatia is the only homeland; he, firing the last shells from the only mortar halted the assault on the fortress at the very instant when some of the attackers had already surmounted the terrace of the fort. Belgrade should also know that it was not only ordinary criminals, in uniform and in civilian clothes, who participated in plunder; but that generals and admirals encouraged the pillage and sometimes even joined in it. (One of them, Admiral Jokić, held until recently the position of Minister of Defence in the Serbian government).

We knew that only wisdom and caution would enable us to confront the Byzantine perfidy in order that the Western tradition of European civilization could be preserved. Life and sacrifice have taught us that caution, wisdom, diplomacy, and money are neither sufficient skills, nor means or devices for defense. We need more: determination, courage, and — unfortunately but certainly — weapons.

National wisdom teaches us that justice travels slowly but arrives eventually. The difficulty is that nobody in Belgrade wants to understand this. Although some are incapable of such understanding, others are not; but either they lack influence, or else those in power are trying to postpone the day — or rather the moment — of their inevitable collapse.

Serbia, with substantial help from its Montenegran satellite, has wounded the old historical heart of the town under Srđ. It has destroyed the area more widely, demolished all its economic potential, and has literally devastated Konavle, Župa, Rijeka, and Primorje. The damages, although they can be registered, are beyond price. The entire population will work to treat the wounds, but the treatment will have to be continued by future generations. The population of the region is imbued with pain and sadness. And not only the Croats. Serbia has slammed upon itself what was before an open door.

Before the world Serbia has disgraced itself and ruined its own credibility — already shaken — because of Dubrovnik. No single foreign diplomat when in contact with anyone from the Serbian or Montenegran leadership or from the so–called "Yugoslav National Army" has failed to blame them or to make a statement about their unforgivable mistake. Lord Carrington and Cyrus Vance have done this, as of course have many others. The Serbian Minister for Foreing Affairs, before a British TV audience, started by trying to deny or to minimalize the damages in Dubrovnik; then he went on hypocritically to deny that any Serbian units were involved in the attacks on Dubrovnik: quite falsely he claimed that the action was carried out by Montenegran reservists alone. Bulatović, who depends upon his leader, had to let this shameful statement pass; he is waiting for the very last moment, if he can catch it, to leave the sinking ship.

The European Twelve were challenged to bring out a special "Declaration on Dubrovnik" on November 8th 1991, which said, *inter alia*, the following:

"The European Community and its member states vigorously condemn the continuing attacks by the JNA on Croatian cities. Agreements about the cease–fire are being violated by all sides, but recent attacks by the JNA are out of all proportion with any action carried out by the Croatian side. In particular, repeated attacks on Dubrovnik have shown, once and for ever, that the statement made by the JNA claiming that its attacks are aimed only to liberate surrounded barracks or to protect Serbian communities, is false.

The JNA declared an ultimatum demanding the actual surrender of Dubrovnik. The European Community and its member states consider this an unlawful act, obviously aimed at conquering this UNDOUBTEDLY CROATIAN TOWN".

53

Thus Serbia *malgré lui* invited, and Dubrovnik because of its own suffering achieved, an explicit Declaration of the European Twelve, one certainly unprecedented in history, that Dubrovnik belongs to Croatia. Let us recall who the Twelve are: France, Great Britain, Germany, Italy, Spain, Portugal, Greece, Holland, Belgium, Luxembourg, Denmark, and Ireland.

This Declaration is not in fact a kind of new discovery. But it gives hidden satisfaction: many of the "scholarly" scribblers from eastern parts of ex–Yugoslavia will be made to realise that all their efforts and money have gone for nothing; and that they should direct their chagrin, with self–criticism, against Milošević and his brethren. They missed the right moment to stop the furious policy proclaimed by their leader on the wings of the Memorandum.

The fact remains that Dubrovnik suffered the worst destruction possible *after* this Declaration of the European Twelve. Possibly as revenge. But another fact is that after the Declaration there have been no more written ultimatums. The enemy has changed his tactics. He is now wanting to break down the defenders by brute force and to kill their desire for defense. He sought assistants to remove the existing Croatian authorities. A psychological war was started against the population, and still continues. However, the enemy has still been beaten by all those who have remained in town, always in their tens of thousands, and their behaviour will be proudly passed down in history.

Facts, pictures, remains, and all the evidence about the dead, about massacres, demolished churches, hospitals, schools etc. in this brutal war are so deeply distressing that really we could not lose this battle. But still all too often in the foreign media the war is still oversimplified, described as a "civil war in Yugoslavia or Croatia", as a "Serbo–Croatian conflict", or as "ethnic confrontations".

We were however unsuccessful when insisting on the communist dimension of the conflict, in particular as it concerned the military. Multiparty democracy is irreconcilable with communism; this element was not successfully presented and used. It is really unforgivable that we did not send throughout the world tens of thousands of copies on the famous "Information by Political Management of the Federal Secretariat for National Defense", dated January 24th 1991, or Adžić's speech on July 6th 1991, or many of Kadijević's performances, or those of Mamula even earlier. We should mention that the communist shadow has never really been pulled–off; it should have been more precisely identified in the substance in which it has prevailed ever since the "Conflict on the Left" of 1940. Well: obviously we did not have enough active individuals engaged in the presentation to the world of this policy, because people who were once infected by communism could not be successful exponents of this very important dimension to the war.

We cannot agree with the argument that the suffering of Dubrovnik brought about the diplomatic recognition of Croatia. Croatia would have been recognised without the sacrifice which Dubrovnik has endured and is still enduring. It would be closer to the truth to say that the suffering of Dubrovnik *accelerated* recognition of Croatia. From Scandinavia to the Pyrenees, even in countries across the ocean, most diplomats talk with extreme indignation about the suffering and the demolition of Dubrovnik. Italian President Cossiga, as the head chief of state who came personally to Croatia to present the credentials of the documents of recognition, said that the calamity of Dubrovnik was, intimately for him, an event which helped ripen his attitude towards the recognition of Croatia. Surely then, Dubrovnik contributed towards speeding up the recognition of Croatia; and proudly, obstinately, but patiently, suffers its own martyrdom.

We are not consoled by the fact that others throughout our only homeland have suffered even more. We are grateful for the help sent from all parts of Croatia and all parts of the free and civilized world that did not abandon us. Croatia must understand that Dubrovnik has been defended by its own citizens, even though not by themselves alone. If anyone doubts that then — before making slanderous remarks — he should look at the list of victims killed in direct battle. A little is known about the nine Yugo–army assaults on the fortress Imperial on Srd. Maybe it is too early to talk of the bravery of Croatian defenders: but in the interests of respect to our admirable youth, and especially because of piety towards those killed in action, it would be distasteful to look for those who are more or less deserving. They fought with weapons in their hands for freedom and an independent Croatia against a more powerful and better–armed enemy.

Dubrovnik is Croatian; and as experience shows, it can survive only as an integral part of that homeland, in view of what it has given to, and received from, Croatia. This is valid for the past, present, and future. But Dubrovnik is, at the same time, unique and special. Everyone who visits sees this: when he gets to know it, he feels it.

All the same, we are aware that talk about Dubrovnik being "special" can have important political connotations: especially when there are certain appeals made by the anonymous or, if not by the anonymous, by those not known for anything good. This concerns particularly the engagement of high–ranking officers in the ex–JNA in the department of "KOS" (the Counterintelligence Service); Colonels Beara and Purlija, now in desperate action throughout the occupied region of Dubrovnik.

It is known that they are trying to play the card of the free Republic of Dubrovnik's tradition: that it should have self–determination, that it is special and precious as the pearl of the whole Slavic south offering a slew of possibilities whereby Dubrovnik would gain particular advantages, have internationally–guaranteed privileges, a special status, etc. In its desperate efforts to hide under the carpet everything it has already done, and at the same time to incorporate Dubrovnik into the spread of its expansionism, Belgrade is offering Dubrovnik autonomy and all the attributes of a federal unit. Yet only the totally naive could neglect the fact that these same authorities would renounce that offer under convenient circumstances.

The writer of these lines had an opportunity, at the end of last October, to meet General Pujić in Belgrade (he was on his way from Zagreb via Vienna and Belgrade to Tivat, then by a gunboat of the occupation army, then by corvette to the old harbour of Dubrovnik; he would take the same route back).

For a conversation conducted in diplomatic language, the dialogue was openminded and direct; and I shall say something about the contents. General Pujić is a doctor of military science, professor at the military academy; he was born in the suburbs of Trebinje, and for decades took his vacations in Kupari. We had no difficulty in agreeing that the bloodshed should be stopped. I expressed sorrow for the large number of dead soldiers and officers in their olive–drab uniforms; my host thought that there were over 450 of these in the areas around Dubrovnik. I emphasised that the grief over the dead defenders of their own native soil, and over civilians throughout Croatia, was even greater.

Pujić showed extreme calm and surprising kindness for a professional soldier, particularly in comparison with what we could see, as we watched them on TV, of generals like Adžić, Negovanović, Aksentijević, Rašeta, Kadijević. He had many words of praise for Dubrovnik's special nature, its traditions, its maritime skill, its cosmopolitanism, its culture, wisdom, diplomacy, and all its other qualities of civilization. Then he directed the conversation towards the chances for Dubrovnik in future conditions. He did not expect that Croatia would succeed in defending itself or in gaining diplomatic recognition, and based his comments on these presuppositions. He said that Dubrovnik should have the independence and autonomy which it had had through its history, and

56

which belonged to it but had been restricted by the contemporary organization of Yugoslavia.

Remembering how Krleža had described a conversation between Supilo and Pašić, I replied to Pujić that recent experiences had confirmed only that every search for a solution within *that* framework were useless. There were some rare persons with such illusions, living too much in the past, who dreamt about an independent Dubrovnik (Kisić, a baker, was prosecuted for that reason in the time of Aleksandar Apolonio, district prosecutor for many years in Dubrovnik, known only for evil). But these dreamers abandoned their utopias when they saw how the waves of populist "antibureaucratic revolution" were quietened down: first in Kosovo, then they had swept off Vojvodina, then left Montenegro mourning. This still communist movement was surrounded by European communism; but was at the same time preparing a requiem for Yugoslavia. Drnovšek, Kučan, Lokar, Stanovnik, Smole, Ribičič, etc. would never have turned their backs on Yugoslavia if Milošević had not appeared on the wings of the "Memorandum". Indeed, as early as August 28th 1991 a respectable British newspaper, *The Guardian,* published an article by Ian Traynor with the title: Milosevic leads Serbia into Wilderness of Paranoia".

General Pujić objected that it was not justifiable to put the army and Milošević on the same footing; but to this I replied emphatically that without entering into a discussion about differences between them, the fact remained that the army had not only kept silent but had also helped Milošević, while at the same time turning its weapons against our youth who used to serve in that very same army, etc.... etc.

My efforts to discuss how military operations and violence might be brought to an end, how a military retreat could be achieved, he declined to take up, giving as an excuse that he was not in the operational, but merely in the political service.

No single answer touched on the issue of Dubrovnik's future; but, ever courteous, he continued his speech about Dubrovnik as a financial and banking centre, a duty–free zone, a centre for multinational companies, etc. To gain persuasiveness he asked me directly: "Why couldn't Dubrovnik enjoy the same status as Monaco, for instance?" I replied very clearly: "Mister General, Monaco's neighbours are the French, and, regretfully, Dubrovnik's are a very different kind of people".

Leaving the Headquarters, which I had been visiting for the first and last time in my life, I remembered the famous sentence: "Beware of the Danaios, even when they bring gifts".

It might be conceded that General Pujić had a candid wish to spare the population of Dubrovnik, provided that some kind of link was accepted with the rest of Yugoslavia. However the Band of Brigands together with all other četnik elements in their brutal war against anything and everything that could be called "Croatian" had more horrifying objectives: by terror and atrocity either to expel, or to exterminate, as many as possible of the present inhabitants and to settle-in Serbs, thereby attaining their expansionist ambitions.

This is indeed one of the most brutal wars ever recorded in history. A conquest of territory: but a territory free of human beings. Do we not have sufficient evidence and warning from Vukovar, Ilok, Dalj, Slunj, Petrinja?

Merit for the survival of Dubrovnik goes first to our boys who have taken up arms to defend their homeland. Eternal thanks and glory to them, in particular to those who gave their lives.

Ending these reflections at a moment when military disentanglement is to be expected, with the obvious internationalization of the retreat of the ex–JNA (and not only from Croatia), it is important for Dubrovnik to remember Dom. Marin's message about the "lion's heart".

History is the teacher of life; but it should be honoured only as one of the important determinants for orientation towards the future. Similarly, historical values depend on all the relevant circumstances of the time. During the last decades in Europe new political and social values have been created, conceived by Schumann, Adenauer, and De Gasperi. As far as future relations between the newly–emerged, recognised and independent states are concerned, the time factor should help to heal the wounds caused by the war. After the inevitable catharsis, tolerance should be substituted for hatred; dialogue and interests of co-existence should prevail over sentiment; and commercial relations should be established — if one wishes to become eligible as a decent partner in the new Europe.

April 1992

The translation was assisted by Kathy Wilkes

Igor Zidić

The Siege of Dubrovnik and the City's Wounds

(Letter to an Italian Friend)

Dear E.,

If you felt relieved watching Yeltsin on your television screen breaking the backbone — with the help of the loyal and democratic Russia — of the Bolshevik coup staged by Yazow and his plotters, I invite you now to turn your attention to the eastern Adriatic shores, to beautiful Dubrovnik, which the famous Arab geographer and travel writer El Idrissi, writing as early as the twelfth century, called the southernmost Croatian coastal city. Look in this direction and you will see the last European partners in crime of the now imprisoned Yazow, Serbian national communists and their (once federal and Tito's) army with assorted gangs of Orthodox fundamentalists, wage their dirty, bloody war against everything that belongs to the civilizational, religious, cultural and political traditions of the Western ecumene. The tragedy of Croatia, both now and in earlier historical periods, stems from its ambiguous, borderline position: for Europe, it is its south*east*, while for Serbia, former Yugoslavia, and the mythic Balkania, it is their north*west*. This is the atavistic, almost mystic–ritual motive for the destruction of Vukovar (not to mention the strategic reasons and territorial aspirations), for the ruination and plunder of Dubrovnik — in short, for the suffering of two cities in the extreme east of northern Croatia and the extreme east of southern Croatia. Dubrovnik has no military, communicational or logistic significance. This makes the irrational motives of its wreckers and their eternal hatred of everything foreign, and superior, all the more transparent. More convincingly than any document, this hatred gives the lie to their empty claims about the Serbian character of Dubrovnik. The two Croatian cities, Vukovar and Dubrovnik, are incarnations of a world that runs counter to the Serbian world and that Serbia finds so odious: this is where the world of the Latin, Catho-

59

lic universalism begins, opposing the parochial religious nationalism; this where, mediated by the aristocracy and religious orders, European cultural standards, forms, conventions and techniques have taken root. It is from these places that the world of work extends in contrast to the world of brigandage; here, rules of parliamentary life apply, there, "dynastic" fights have been the rule, compounded by political murders. Do I need to remind you — no matter what we might think about the Austrian Monarchy — that Serbia and its secret organizations (The Black Hand, Unity or Death, Young Bosnia) acted as a firing pin on the trigger of the Russian gun and ultimately, with the assassination of Prince Ferdinand, directly caused the outbreak of the First World War? This was the war of many against many, but for Orthodox, semi–asiatic Russia and its Orthodox Balkan satellite this was a war against the Catholic, Central European Danubian civilization, against Austria–Hungary, and against the European institutions.

I am telling you all these things hoping that you will understand that the present war against Croatia is a war against everything that was, and is, European, democratic and Catholic in what was once Yugoslavia. I do not, of course, wish to imply that only what is Catholic is European or democratic, but I would like to stress that these are the three concepts that the traditional Serbian politics — Orthodox, authoritarian and populist — has viewed as embodiments of Satan and the Ennemy. (Until quite recently, the Serbo–Communist Party leadership used to brand every more prominent Croatian Communist who refused to toe the Party line as an "agent of the Vatican".)

That is why, it seems to me, the Croatian politicians make a mistake when, for pragmatic reasons, they try to gloss over the historical, and even mythical, irrational motives and aspects of this horrible war, fearing its possible political minorization (as a "tribal conflict") by the great powers. In order to make it easier for the Americans to understand the issues and for the sluggish Europe to come to a decision more quickly, the Croatian government insists that this is merely an ideological war between paleo–communists and bolsheviks on the Serbian side and Euro–democrats on the Croatian side. It was only when the development of the war operations at last made the geopolitical aims of the Serbian oligarchy visibly plain even to the most naive observers, and when the occupying troops had captured almost a third of Croatia's territory, that it was officially recognized that what we were witnessing was a *war of two states* — Serbia against Croatia. But even at this stage we are still concealing the fact that — in addition to the war just mentioned — there is another one that is being waged on Croatian soil, namely, a *civil war* waged by a part of the Serbian population in Croatia against their native land, its institutions and all its citizens, including Serbs, who love it and are loyal to it. For the time being, we are also concealing the fact that an *ethnic war* is going on here, aimed at decimating the Croatian population, especially in areas which Serbia openly claims for itself. This is seen not only in the large numbers of people in many towns and villages who have been driven from their homes or killed, but also in the destruction of numerous historic monuments and works of art, civilizational and cultural heritage, irreplaceable evidence of centuries of Croatian existence and source of national self–awareness. By killing people, not even sparing children, destroying homes, factories, roads and bridges, closing the national airspace and blockading sea ports, the Serbian army is trying to deny our present existence and to deprive us of our future. But by destroying our historic heritage — particularly in the historically vital region of Croatian Dalmatia, in Zadar, Šibenik, Split, and Dubrovnik — Serbia is trying to defeat us retroactively in our past: it is intent on erasing our historical memory and eliminating us from the consciousness of other nations. Thus, this is not just a war between states but also ethno–genocide, a war against the entire natural and cultural heritage of this country. Make no mistake: this is a war against everything that international conventions are designed to protect — hospitals, wounded people, medical staff, ambulance vehicles, schools and kindergartens, civilians, cultural monuments, museums, archives, libraries, and the human environment. This is a war in the best tradition of the Serbian "Black Hand" criminal policy: a total war, stabbing into the opponent's body and soul, his past and present. This, whether we like to recognize it or not, is also a *religious war* against other, non–Orthodox religions. The most telling proof of this are the tree fingers raised as a symbol of Orthodoxy by the Serbian and Montenegrin raiders and assailants, as well as the many shattered, burnt, desecrated and demolished Catholic churches, molested and murdered priests, bombarded Jewish cemeteries, staged "Ustashe" subversion acts, heavily shelled synagogue in Dubrovnik, and great Moslem casualties.

All of these *wars* together, dear E., make up this "small" war on the outskirts of Europe, for which Comrade Gorbachov — the same Gorbachov who returned to the political arena thanks to the good will of Mr. Yeltsin — is supplying oil, filling the fuel tanks of the armoured vehicles commanded by the Serbian Yazow and his Yazowites. The same example is already being followed by Romania. So much for the international embargo on exports of strategic commodities to Yugoslavia and for the Allied lobbying! Croatia is being upbraided for receiving support from Germany (and a few other Western countries), while Serbia can freely accept the helping hand of the Soviet Union and Romania. *Sapienti sat*.

What can Dubrovnik expect in this nightmarish torment? The ruthless and primitive Serbian army, asiatically cruel, communist indoctrinated, wildly fanatical in their Orthodoxy and displaying Levantine duplicity in negotiation surrounds this city, which is ours and yours, like a serpent. Dubrovnik is one of the symbols of ancient Europe and one of the deep roots of our Mediterranean origins. It is also an age–old metropolis of Croatian culture, first a commune and then a republic, which developed its "state of law and order" from the Middle Ages on, asserting the spirit of work and orderly living, in contradistinction to the disorderly chaos of the eastern, Byzantine–Serbian and Turkish, hinterland. In contrast to the obscure Balkan market towns and brigands' holes, Dubrovnik was a model of an ideal city. It separated from the dark and threatening forests and wild gorges of the distant hinterland by a belt of Arcadian harmony. Dubrovnik is a carefully built and carefully landscaped city. It is a city with a long and rich Catholic tradition, the home of preachers and of the religious orders that promoted schoolarship and architecture — Benedictines, Franciscans, Dominicans, Jesuits. Dubrovnik is a city — and an expression — of the cosmopolitan, peaceful, maritime, hardworking, educated and cultured Croatia, the birthplace of great scientists and scholars, writers, sea captains, entrepreneurs, excellent cartographers, and engineers. And despite its historically justified cautiousness, it has always been a very open city, with a Mediterranean atmosphere, with excellent commercial and maritime communications, and displaying full religious and national tolerance. It was neither servile nor xenophobic. It was the home of German craftsmen, Greek and Spanish scholars, Italian physicians, lawyers and artists, painters and architects. It was the home of people coming from all over Croatia and from many parts of Italy. It was also the Frontier: Light on the Borders of Darkness. *Dubrovnik is everything that Serbia is not.* It is a mirror that faithfully reflects Serbia's historical remoteness and its present ugliness. Those that claim Dubrovnik as their own from a distance, bombard it from close quarters, thus demonstrating that they have found nothing in it that is theirs. The inferno that now surrounds Dubrovnik, the fires that engulf it, the shells that destroy it — all these are just a futile attempt to turn Croatia's most beautiful scenes of harmony into a wasteland, to make it resemble Serbia more closely. Many invaders — before the Serbs and Montenegrins — have destroyed foreign cities and homes. But none of them have so far built a home for themselves on bombs. The spirit of robbery does not reside in Dubrovnik: in order to capture the city, the robber must destroy it, and once destroyed the city ceases to be the robber's obsessive irrational aim. That is why Serbia is actually closing to itself the door that it is trying to force open. Throughout Croatia, particularly in Slavonia and Dalmatia, Serbia has effectively uprooted itself forever. The Serbian army may still destroy many targets, but it cannot build anything. That is why it cannot, and will not, enter Dubrovnik.

(By night 25th November 1991)

Translated by Vladimir Ivir

Ivo Frangeš

The Presence of Dubrovnik

"I dreamed of being at sea... Paris woke me up." This is how Paul Valéry begins his impressive evocation of Paris under the title *"Présence de Paris"*. Everything that the human ear, awake or asleep, can hear in Paris boils down to the experience of an expanse of sea. "Je rêvais d'être en mer...". And then, while listing all the numberless sounds, noises, roars, bellowing of mechanical forces putting pressure on the matter, Valéry wants to imagine Paris: "Penser Paris".

"Penser Dubrovnik". What must a person experience, hear, sea in order to begin to think about Dubrovnik, "to think Dubrovnik". A miraculous city in which the sounds mentioned by Valéry are narrowed down, minimized, excluded... Even the sea, on which Dubrovnik seems to sail as a mythical carrack, can hardly be heard in the central square — the Placa. What can be heard is neither the scream of nature, nor the screeching of wheels, nor the clash of engines, nor the noise of the endless mass of people. "Penser Dubrovnik" is the image of a magic vessel full of bursts of needle–like twitters of swallows, the bang of an occasional window suddenly shut, the unique dialogue of the church–bells, and the unrepeated melody of the language. This same mine and your Croatian language is realized in a particular Dubrovnik manner, being at once a poem and a tradition, recalling simultaneously Šiško and Džore, Marin and Dživo*, and reminding that talking means putting together words, sounds and melodies belonging to the ancient and eternally alive but also to those who are coming and who, by using the same language, will remember us. How to think Paris? How to express the values produced by the efforts of a great nation? — asks Valéry, Paris, the seat of beauty and anxiety, the goal of so many travellers and the desire of so many conquerors? To think Dub-

---

*   Šiško Menčetić, Džore Držić, Marin Držić, Dživo Gundulić, famous literary figures of Dubrovnik.

Željko Šoletić / The Residence Skočibuha — the Scientific Library, June 8, 1992

Milo Kovač / Dubrovnik cemetery (Boninovo), November 1991

Pavo Urban / Consequences of the war in the City Harbour,
November 1991

Pavo Urban / Ship »Iverak«, Port of Gruž, November 27, 1991

Pavo Urban / Rescuing the ship »Adriatic II«, port of Gruž,
November 1991

Matko Biljak / Dubrovnik landscape — the port Gruž, November 1991

Matko Biljak / **Motif from Dubrovnik, Port of Gruž, November 1991**

Milo Kovač / St. Anne's church in Brgat (near Dubrovnik), October 14, 1991

Božidar Đukić / Devastation of the building of the Inter–University Centre, December 6, 1991

Željko Šoletić / The destroyed and burnt–out library of the Inter–University Centre (25,000 volumes), December 6, 1991

Željko Šoletić / Inter–University Centre, December 6, 1991

Milo Kovač / **Destruction of the port of Gruž, November 1991**

Milo Kovač / Restaurant of the Hotel »Libertas«, December 6, 1991

Milo Kovač / **The market–place in Gruž, November 1991**

rovnik, its stone slabs on the rocks, its rocks on the cliffs, its Srđ trying in vain to surmount it, its sea trying in vain to undermine it? Earthquakes do sometime shake it but never manage to destroy it. It is only human mindlessness that could feel its spiteful and undestructible beauty a challenge.

To think Dubrovnik... its inhabitants in clash and in harmony, in collision and in love shedding a common tear to water the fresh scars of their city. Paris may stand the march of heavily armed soldiers; they will be soon forgotten by its buildings and squares. A military march on the Dubrovnik Placa is an absurd nonsense. The small but eternal Dubrovnik could be harmed only from distance; the brutal hand lacks the courage to touch the bastions of liberty but does it indirectly aiming from far away.

Among the World's Babels — Valéry says — Paris is the most personal, the most diversified, it is a peculiar kind of political and industrial centre, the market and the point of convergence of numerous values; it is not only an artificial paradise and a centre of culture but all that simultaneously. Every Frenchman who takes himself seriously is devoted to Paris because it is the head of France.

Dubrovnik, the small and miraculous Dubrovnik, is not like that: it is neither an industrial nor a financial centre, it is not an intersection of important routes, it is not even an artificial garden. It is a beauty on the rock, it is gaiety on the edge of an abyss, it stands for the reliance on the human hand and for a witness to the power of the mind. It is the victory of the intellect over dullness, it is an eternal banner of freedom, the freedom of the spirit and of the body. When a Croatian person — with hope and pride — thinks of himself, of his ways and his indebtedness, he thinks about Dubrovnik. That is that permanent presence of Dubrovnik in ourselves and in the world. "La présence de Dubrovnik". The presence of the Croatian Athens which today, in December of 1991, foolish heads and brutal hands are trying to push into the sea. In vain.

Translated by Damir Kalogjera

Kathleen V. Wilkes

Jus in bello

Act so that you treat humanity, whether in your own person or in that of another, always as an end and never as a means only. (Kant. Foundations of the Metaphysics of Morals, 2nd section.)

Just Wars and Crimes of War

The question whether it is possible to start a "just" war — the question of "jus ad bellum" — is one which provokes and should provoke much thought. I believe that there have been some such wars, in the past; but in the Europe of the 1990s it is difficult to think of adequate justification for initiating a war. All of us have been forced to wonder about this, over the last year.

It is worth noting that the Treaty of London declared it criminal for anyone to plan, prepare, and initiate a war in violation of treaties, agreements, and assurances: and virtually every nation is signatory to a treaty that rejects war as a policy–instrument. The UN General Assembly in 1974 asserted that aggression is "the most serious and dangerous form of the illegal use of force". The same Assembly, however, allowed "the inherent right of individual or collective self–defense if an armed attack occurs...". so the defenders can be fighting a "just" war against aggressors fighting an unjust one.

However, the problem of whether there are now any just wars of aggression or intervention, although independently absorbing, will not be my concern here. Moreover, anyone reading this will be thinking first and foremost of the war of aggression against Croatia and Bosnia–Herzegovina, the manifest injustice of which needs no discussion.

For, even if that question, the "jus ad bellum" question, has been adequately answered, even if the war is called "just", another remains: what methods of warfare are morally legitimate: what about "jus in bello"? It is of course oversimple to separate the two issues as sharply as I have just done: if a country is at fault for initiating a war (if the attack itself contravenes national and international principles of moral legitimacy) then of course any actions taken by the belligerent will be unjustifiable — as we have seen for ourselves, here in Croatia. Indeed, we could go further: Melzer has suggested that a just war (jus ad bellum) conducted in an unjust way (jus in bello) becomes unjust (jus ad bellum): the jus ad bellum might be "anchored" in the jus in bello (Y. Melzer, *Concepts of Just war*, Leyden, 1975, p. 87–93). Well: whatever we make of that interesting suggestion, we can look at the second question on the supposition that the aggressor is justified in his aggression: for what is morally indefensible in a "just" war will be doubly so in an unjust one.

I shall present two prima facie rival theories that purport to describe what does or does not count as a crime of war (actions that contravene the jus in bello): and then will go on to explore some of the implications of this distinction.

Two Moral Theories

The history of moral and political philosophy reveals, again and again, a tension between two major intuitions. One, broadly, we might call "Kantian", "deontological", or "absolutist". The other is consequentialism. (I hope that the jargon–labels are not too off–putting; I shall try to sketch the two theories in a clear way). There is great difficulty in describing these two rival intuitions so that there is a clear distinction between them: but exploring the ambiguities, unclarities, and implications of both will help us with the main issue, the issue of war crimes. I shall start by sketching both in rough outline.

The first view, the "Kantian" view, emphasises what is done, rather than what will result from the doing. Actions in and of themselves can be good or evil, no matter what their consequences may be: some actions are simply banned. Perhaps the Catholic "doctrine of double effect" illustrates this most clearly (although it itself is not unproblematic). This doctrine claims a morally relevant distinction between, say, killing an innocent person deliberately (either because his death is the goal, or because killing him will help bring about a wanted goal): and killing him as a foreseeable side–effect of another action which one does deliberately. In the first case, killing him is regarded as evil. In the second case, it is regarded as a regrettable, unwanted, but unfortunately inevitable, side–effect of the action that is performed, and may be excused, or even required, if the action of which it is a side–effect was demanded.

Examples would help. Imagine yourself at the top of a hill in a car where gears and brakes have failed. The car is out of control: at the bottom of the hill the road forks. To the right is a single unwary pedestrian: to the left, five. Most people would agree that you should wrench the steering–wheel to take the right–hand fork — even though this will kill the person in your path — rather than turn left and kill five. The death of the one is predictable, regrettable, unwanted; but was not your aim: if you could have avoided it, you would have done so. Contrast this with a case — and there have been such situations — where five people would starve to death unless they killed and ate a sixth person. In this second example the death of one is a means to the end of the survival of the five. This, for the Kantian, would be impermissible.

These examples, as so often in moral philosophy, are extreme: but they serve as "intuition pumps" to clarify the difference in question.

Consequentialism, by contrast, claims that the rightness or wrongness of any action depends upon the goodness or badness of its consequences. Thus it entails the following plausible principle: if you have the opportunity to prevent a great evil but at the cost of bringing about a lesser evil, then you are morally obliged to bring about, or permit, the lesser evil. So deliberately killing, say, civilians in war would be in some extreme circumstances justifiable, if by doing so the war were to be brought rapidly to an end — perhaps because the enemy became demoralised, perhaps because there was an internal revolution. The deaths of a few, or even many, noncombatant civilians would be evil, certainly; but the greater number of military and civilian deaths that would accompany a longer war would be a more appalling evil still. This was one of the arguments used in the attempt to defend the Hiroshima bombing in the Second World War: as also the bombing of Hamburg, Amsterdam, Coventry, Dresden. Closer to home: radio Titograd repeatedly asked Dubrovnik to surrender for reasons related to this: more devastation and death would be averted, the radio said, if the city surrendered.

Necessary hostility

We must now turn to consider some of the difficulties in drawing a sharp distinction between these two prima facie opposing theories, particularly in the case of crimes of war. For one thesis upon which both would undoubtedly agree is that violence of any kind against the enemy — whether combatant or not, whether against him or against his property — is unjustifiable when it is not necessary for victory. So, for instance, raping or looting by an occupying army, since it brings about no military advantage, cannot be justified: nor can the wanton targetting and destruction of property or of cities, towns, and villages, the bombing of hospitals and cemeteries, the ill–treatment of prisoners or of an occupied population. Indeed, the Hague Convention in the 1920s concluded that "aerial bombardment destined to terrorize the civilian population, or to destroy or damage private property which has no military character, or to wound noncombatants, is prohibited". Later, the International Military Tribunal at Nuremberg included in their definition of "crimes against humanity" the following: ... ill treatment or deportation to slave labour or for any other purpose of civilian population of or in occupied territory,... plunder of public or private property, wanton destruction of cities, towns, or villages, or devastation not justified by military necessity. (*Trials of the Major War Criminals Before the International Military Tribunal*, 22, 1948)

It is evident that the "Kantian" position would forbid all such activities; but so, very often, would an enlightened consequentialism: such behaviour is very likely to militate against a satisfactory victory, since it would probably bring about hatred and resentment, thus constituting a future military liability. (The allies' destruction of Hamburg in the Second World War was a case in point: although "justified" as a retaliation for the destruction of Amsterdam and Coventry, it backfired against the allies: the German population was outraged, and workers formerly working in industries unrelated to the aims of the war were freed to move into war–related industries. A local example: when a Serbian apologist (Nora Beloff) claimed, in a letter to *The Times* of London, that the assault upon Croatia could be explained by the "fact" that Croatia was discriminating against Serbs, Uwe Kitzinger dryly commented in a letter to the same paper that bombing civilians was a poor way of persuading them to be more tolerant.)

Self–Deception and Justification

A second difficulty in drawing a clear distinction between a tenable form of absolutism and a sophisticated form of consequentialism is of particular interest — both for the topic of war crimes, and for the attempt to understand something of how people can commit them. There is the brute fact that "the same" actions can be described in a whole range of ways. As Bertrand Russell put it, we like to say such things as "I am firm: you are obstinate; he is pig-headed". We choose the description that suits our self-image best. Take a real-life case: Wilkes Booth's assassination of Lincoln. If what he did is (truthfully) described as "firing a gun", then there is nothing intrinsically wrong with that; with that description, it is indeed the consequences of the action that make it wrong. But he could also be described, again truthfully, as "murdering Lincoln". Here it is not the consequences that make his action wicked: murder, if seen as the intentional killing of an innocent man, is as such wrong, wrong in itself — not because of its consequences (bad though they may also be). Wilkes Booth, for his part, might believe that a true description of his action was "freeing the country of a tyrant" ("sic semper tyrannis!"), which would be a description of an action which is, as so described, good. And so on.

Thus, if the bombing and destruction of a village, involving the deaths of civilians, is described as a means to the end of killing the combatant soldiers who are also there, the absolutist would reject such a course of action and the consequentialist might accept it; but the same bombing could be described as "obliterating a haven for the enemy combatants", and civilian deaths might then be seen as a foreseeable but unwanted side-effect — in which case the absolutist, as well as the consequentialist, might accept it. To take, again, an example close to home: we have seen, over and over, the deliberate bombardment of Croatian churches: when "justified" at all, the excuse is that there was or might have been a Croatian sniper or machine gun in the tower (an excuse that fell flat in the case of the church at Brgat, near Dubrovnik, which had no tower). So the selected description is not "destroying a church", but "attacking snipers".

This, I believe, is the strategy that soldiers very often have to use, in order to live with themselves after engaging in such atrocities as these: to hang on to some minimal sense of integrity. The strategy is: select that description which makes what you have done a good thing to do ("attacking snipers", "freeing the country of a tyrant"); reject the one that shows it to be a war crime ("destroying a church", "murdering a great statesman"). It is self-deception via selection of action-description. Self-deception is very strongly motivated — it is a pressing human demand to picture oneself to oneself in the best light possible. The carefully chosen description is not an attempt to mitigate, or to excuse, the act: the act itself is not portrayed as in need of either. The attempt is to justify, to claim that the deed was a right thing to do.

Evidently, this is where the role of national propaganda comes in most strongly. Probably the Montenegran soldier in occupied Mokošica really believed what he said when he explained to a friend of mine — while standing in front of the four blackened walls that were all that was left of a house in Mokošica — why he could not yet go home, even though the Geneva agreement of November 23rd had been signed: he said to her: "but we still haven't liberated Dubrovnik!" Radio Titograd had been telling him for weeks of the need to "liberate" Dubrovnik. "Occupying" versus "liberating"... national media naturally try to make life easier for their own troops, by giving them a description of their activities with which they can live.

"Contractual" Considerations: Justification and Relevance

I turn to a third dimension in which it is hard to sketch a clear difference between the two rival moral/political theories, in the case of war crimes. The Kantian claim with which I began this essay is one which it is hard to contest. It has very strong intuitive appeal. Indeed, consequentialists of a certain stripe might also accept it as a fundamental principle. I am thinking here of so–called "contractual" consequentialists. (I apologise for this bit of jargon: I think it will be easy to explain.) Such thinkers would borrow from John Rawls the idea — admittedly a "thought experiment", not any historical or possible event — that political principles, and principles of morality, should be such as would be agreed–upon by rational agents who were meeting in a position of ignorance about their own actual position in society: ignorant of their age, health, sex, income, marital status, race, religion, etc. In such an imaginary situation, Rawls argues, they are likely to agree upon principles that they would be prepared to see adopted for cases in which they might themselves be at the receiving–end, in which they might be the ones who lost–out. Thus, for example, slavery would be outlawed, because those debating the structure of society would not know whether they would prove to be slaves or masters, and so rational self–interest would prohibit them from taking the risk of approving a slave–owning society. More generally, it would be difficult for the contractualist to accept the risk that he might be the one to suffer, or to be sacrificed for the welfare of others without his consent. Put another way, in a quasi–Kantian way, prudence would require anyone behind the "veil of ignorance" to regard all others as "ends in themselves", if he himself wanted to be so treated.

The analogy of Rawls' "veil of ignorance" for war would be the various Hague Conventions: real meetings, not thought–experimental ones. Those conventions, after all, were attended by representatives of various nations, all taking seriously the possibility that their nations might at some time be at war. Then, aware of their common humanity and with a calculated eye to their national self–interest, but behind a veil of ignorance of whether, when, or with what other nation, they might some day be at war, and of how such a war would develop, they sought to frame "rules of war". Thus national self–interest can explain why these conventions attempt to prohibit looting, attacking civilian residences, hospitals, schools, religious buildings, cultural monuments: and to outlaw germ or chemical warfare, the use of napalm, the taking of hostages, the ill–treatment of prisoners (whether combatant or non–combatant).

Wars are, it is trivial to say, engagements between people. It is perfectly possible to take hostile actions against others while acknowledging that they are "ends in themselves"; and this both the Kantian and the "consequentialist contractualist" picture demand. It is possible therefore to hate or resent an enemy, to take actions against him, while acknowledging the humanity he shares with you?

If we accept this, then an associated principle, again difficult to refute, comes into play. Although there is rarely any need to "justify" friendly actions taken on behalf of others (although some such actions might be puzzling things to do — "why are you going to such lengths to help him?" — and so in need of explanation), acting in a way that harms them needs both explanation and justification. And reason demands that explanation and justification highlight, and appeal to, the features relevant to the response. So, for example, the hair colour of another is very rarely relevant to any action taken for or against him: nor his height; nor the make of his car. Hostile actions, resentment, hatred, are justified (if at all) by features specific to the person in question in those circumstances: and it is in terms of these features that, say, shooting or killing might be rationally defensible. The object of hostile actions is the feature of the agent that provoked the response. So not his race, religion, age, health; let alone eye–colour or make of car. A combination of the "veil of ignorance" principle, and the "relevant justification" principle, shows clearly how so many of the attacks against Croatia can count as war crimes.

If so: then, to take a different example, spreading scandal about a political opponent — such as the attempts in the 1992 Presidental primaries in the US to smear Clinton with gossip about sex scandals — could not be justified. This is because, except to the rigid puritan, past sexual misdemeanours are irrelevant to the reason for the opposition: that reason being his challenge to your preferred candidate's chances of getting the nomination. Justifiable hostile activity must take the form of an attack on political ability, publicising past political misjudgments, even perhaps casting doubt upon his political integrity. It is necessary to direct the attack on that which makes him the target of your hostility.

How does this affect permissible activities in war? Clearly, if an enemy is bombing your position, it is for most non–pacifists justifiable to try to shoot him, if there is no other way of stopping him. Your attack is directed very specifically against an enemy whose actions against you, or your troops, present a very real threat. This, as I have argued, is entirely compatible with treating him as an end in himself rather than as a means — both hating and loving are "I–thou" relationships, after all. (This however needs an important qualification. In contemporary warfare the combatants need not see, or even be within miles of, each other. Psychologically speaking, it must be easier to forget or ignore the humanity of the opposing troops when they cannot be seen. This too we have seen in the war against Croatia: boats and rockets bombed Dubrovnik from over the horizon, as well as from close by.) Although it may be justifiable to try to kill an aggressor, it would not be justifiable to take his wife and children hostage and threaten to kill them unless he stops; nor to bomb a nearby civilian village belonging to his side to distract him from the assault upon your troops; nor to torture him once he was captured. Taking hostages is — as we have seen in the Lebanon — treating people as means; so is the destruction of people and property who have not provoked such actions; torturing a prisoner treats him as a means to the end of vengeance, or perhaps information.

But this argument need not necessarily commit one to the "absolutist" position. For even if the Kantian demand is not accepted in its strongest form, the point (which appeals only to what counts as rational justification) that actions must be explained or defended by citing relevant features of the agent or of the situation will remain. Hostile actions must be justified; and they can be justified only when they are directed against the causes of the danger. And this remains true, note, even when the attacker is a reluctant and morally innocent conscript, forced against his will to fight: and the noncombatant is morally evil and an ardent supporter of his side. For the purpose of justifiable killing in self–defense, the noncombatant is innocent of the aggression which alone justifies the retaliation: to kill him would go beyond what can be defended. (The morally guilty noncombatant may need to be punished. But that is not the role of self–defense. In Zagreb, where I presented a version of this paper, I was asked to give an example of a "morally guilty noncombatant" in the war against Croatia. Professor Supek came to my rescue: the infamous SANU document, and hence the Serbian Academicians.)

"Relevance" is all–important when considering war crimes. During a war, every nation has to engage itself in most of the activities that belong equally to peace: feeding the population, caring for the sick, educating its citizenry, allowing for religious observance, providing energy, transport systems, and so on. Since these activities are neutral as between war and peace, they cannot be cause or pretext for hostile action to disrupt or disturb them. Certainly food is required to sustain the enemy forces, and hospitals to heal their wounds (and maybe thereafter enable them to return to the attack). But since food and medical care are needed by people qua people, and not qua aggressive enemy troops, hospitals, farms and forests, power–plants, transport systems are not legitimate targets: blockades and sieges are not legitimate strategies — even if a blockade may force a city to surrender, thus perhaps shortening the war. It is not because the enemy is a person (and thus needs food and medical care) that he can be attacked: it is because of what he is doing qua soldier.

Similarly, certain kinds of weaponry have to be outlawed. Clearly a bullet kills the person as well as the soldier; but it is qua soldier that such killing might be justifiable. Weapons that disfigure, or burn (like napalm), or inflict disease (like germ warfare) injure him qua man. It may seem paradoxical that killing an opponent may in some circumstances be justifiable, whereas disfiguring him or inflicting burns on him is not. But deliberately to disfigure an individual cannot be justified by any hostile action against of his; not even if he has used such weapons against your side. This point is related to the fact that both sides should be limited to the means necessary for overcoming the opponent; we need to look at both necessity, and relevance.

Concluding pessimistic postscript

I have made this sound all too simple. Few if any absolute prohibitions cannot be overridden in exceptional circumstances; anyone can dream–up a situation in which some atrocities seem at least pardonable, if not "justifiable": when, for instance, a nation is threatened with annihilation. Oppenheim remarks that if the basic values of society are threatened, nations are possibly released from all restrictions and prohibitions in order to do what "they deem to be decisive for the ultimate vindication of the law of nations" (*International Law*, p. 251).

The brute fact is that from time to time people are confronted with an appalling choice between two morally reprehensible courses of action; and whatever they do will, they might think, be evil. Washing one's hands, like Pilate, can at times be reprehensibly self–indulgent. Against that we can only say that either: not all moral dilemmas are soluble — a gloomy, but possibly true, conclusion; or that feeling guilty, even if psychologically unavoidable, is not the same as being guilty. Sinning is not the same as having the sense of being a sinner: moral integrity is not the same as peace of mind. This response is perhaps a greater consolation. Fortunately, though, such situations are exceptional. Usually we are worse than we think we are — see the discussion of self–deception above: just occasionally we are better.

Tonko Maroević

Dubrovnik Besieged

The beauty of Dubrovnik is not due to a chance or a whim, neither has it been extortioned by excessive aesthetic ambitions nor by the overwhelming will of a single project. On the contrary. It is the result of a very sober consideration of the state and of the ambience including pragmatic appreciation of the conditions and necessities. What is more, it represents the result of a systematic accumulation of age–long experience and of economical utilization of the gathered insights. Dubrovnik is beautiful the way a shell or a wal–nut are beautiful, and perfect as a precious stone or a watch mechanism when free of anything redundant or unnecessary.

The miracle of Dubrovnik is not of a natural origin and even less so of the supernatural. Behind that unrepeatable crystalization stand the generations of its inhabitants and the brilliant historical structure, though powerful and majestic, it has preserved its human measure. This city was built for the purpose of living and gathering within its walls but primarily for the defence against the outside danger from unsympathetic competitors and envious neighbours. Dubrovnik has therefore been since its very beginning a stronghold, a complex of strong walls and a closed fortification system. Its forts and bastions had not only endured the numerous attacks, they had also discouraged the most powerful armies of the time, those of the Serenissima and the Ottoman Empire. The enormous diplomatic skill and a tendency towards copromise of the old Dubrovnik citizens may have been their most precious weapon not to mention their craftiness and the offering of bribes, but still defensive walls had to be there to impress the potential aggressor and to make him re–examine his plans of the possible conquest. The freedom of Dubrovnik has been built into its very foundations and has shaped its roofs and cupolas. Ironically, its fortifications which followed closely the contemporary strategic and ballistic achievements have practically remained unused throughout the long periods of pre–technological warfares to show its paradoxical functionality during the attack of the unbridled Yugoslav Army and incited Serbo–Montenegrin reservists. One must also mention here the purely brigand mentality of the hillbillies from the surrounding mountains who, like two hundred years ago, have used the presence of sympathetic aggressors (at the beginning of the 19th century it was the Russians) to loot the City and its surroundings.

The earlier episode was, however, of a limited size and duration. This time Dubrovnik has been besieged, destroyed, exposed to exhaustion, its inhabitants killed for a long time. For the first time it has been reduced to the life *intra muros* which had not happened even in times of epidemics or catastrophic earthquakes, as its skillful foreign policy was capable of neutralizing the danger of internal isolation or direct threats of the restless neighbourhood.

It is tragic that the life of Dubrovnik has been brought in question by those who should be grateful to that city for helping them step out on the historical scene and come closer to the developed world. This city had known how to establish links both with famous centres of culture and with the anonymous backwoods in its Balkan hinterland. There is no doubt that these latter links were forged with commercial goals in mind but nevertheless the move had helped the spread of culture in these poor areas so that both individuals and social groups have risen to a new civilizational level and had left written traces. Good parts of Herzegovina, Montenegro, Kosovo, Sandžak, Serbia and Bosnia have entered the world trade via this city about which there are countless documents in their Archives.

The experienced and clever ruling group, however, did not permit excessive fraternizing with the neighbouring people and had placed the religious filter as the condition for any assimilation, thus eliminating members of other religions from settling down in the City with the limited exception of the cosmopolitan Jews.

The old Dubrovnik citizens had intuitively had much less confidence in Byzantium influenced neighbouring rulers than the Islamic world with which they established such balance of interests that it could serve as an example even for the present. And indeed, it has been shown that it is the closest neighbours that cause most trouble and that neither gratefulness may be expected from the envious nor understanding from those who are only prepared to grab without investing or contributing.

We do not mean to say that Dubrovnik had found it easy to deal with the West and that it was joyously met by the brethren in language and faith. It jealously preserved its independence against any moves particularly from the side of the (also byzantinized) Venice and her vassal lands in the closer neighbourhood. Ironic attitudes towards the inhabitants of Korčula and Kotor, for example, besides their campanilistic spirit, point towards a certain political reservation for reasons of state. On the other hand, everything that reached the city from the other side of the sea, from the Mediterranean, was accepted lightly and fitted organically and logically into the fabric of local life. Dubrovnik welcomed the guests from Hvar and Zadar, Senj and Zagreb not to mention the master craftsmen from Florence, Rome, Bari and merchants from Genoa, Marseille and Barcelona.

Owing to the unshakeable universalism of its Catholic formation, Dubrovnik had easily communicated with the Hungarian–Croatian state and relied on it as on a guarantor and protector in strategically difficult situations. Through their mentality, customs and literary work the citizens of Dubrovnik had established narrow contacts with their co–nationals on the same coast realizing that they may reckon with a special position in this company owing to their special status as the most modern and most developed centre. Dubrovnik has grown into Croatian tradition and culture but has always rightly retained a certain distinctivness since it has been the most complete and most distinguished model of civilization, harmony and subtlety.

The city which used to be dubbed Croatian Athens and which was looked at with admiration by the Dalmatian islands and communes, which was celebrated by Hektorović, and Lucić, Mažuranić, Šenoa, Miletić and Gavella as the source of their inspiration is now being bombarded by those who have no affective relation towards it nor intellectual understanding of it but, aware that they cannot own it, have developed only the complex of jealousy and envy. If they cannot have it, they show clearly, they can destroy it. Since it does not and cannot belong to them, they want to take it by force from those to whom it does belong, from those who live in and for the city and have inherited it from their ancestors as an obligation and a promise, as their fate and their future.

The exceptional role of Dubrovnik can be understood only by those who feel it in depth and who can see that in the final summing up it has delivered more and better. Only those who love and respect it, to whom it is necessary and who are its legitimate inheritors, those who speak in favour of peace and liberty, who defend work and harmony, only they deserve Dubrovnik. The attackers have definitively shown that they have nothing to do with it, that they have not learned the lesson from the City's beneficial influence.

How to end this gloomy text? Dubrovnik has been under siege for some months now and, while it endures the hardships, it has nevertheless suffered irreparable losses, injuries, traumas, deaths, disappointments, defeatism and apathy. There is little hope that these sufferings will be soon relieved and particularly those inflicted to the surrounding countryside without which Dubrovnik cannot breathe. These are neither the times for boasting nor for threatening. This is the time for utilising all the internal power coming from the long experience of wise moves in the past and the hope in the salvation will show up. Let us believe that the council of the besieged will reach the level of the historical Small and Grand Councils and find the way out of this impasse.

Translated by Damir Kalogjera

Zvonimir Mrkonjić

The Burnt Land

The Walls of Dubrovnik

Dubrovnik has for centuries lived encircled by a riddle, its walls. It is well known that the walls had never had to defend the city from direct attack, because as much as the attack was expected, it actually never happened. The walls defended Dubrovnik mostly from time, from the violence of its onset: Everything that passed through the City Gates were able to change any temporary features, but not the City's shell, not its concept. Built for a well known purpose, the walls have eventually become firmly established, as Antun Šoljan[1] would say "for an unknown purpose". Dubrovnik thus floated through time on its stone sailing ship. Vojnović[2] however complained that it could not cut loose from its mainland. It sailed through imperial wars which shattered against its walls while the walls were hardened even more. Whoever entered the City was impressed most by the walls that defined the lands where Freedom had been defended. Everything else was on the other side of the walls. All liberators withdrew in the face of the power of Freedom, the only force that could deliver them from themselves. The walls remained standing like a riddle and a warning: Has the purpose of the walls' existence only been suspended? Has it therefore been only the more relentless? Invaders appeared one day in the territories of Dubrovnik. Their aims were made public long ago, but nobody believed that they could be fulfilled — unless in the milennial anticipation of Doomsday. Since the invaders had no means to force the City to surrender without fighting, they began a siege, cutting off vital supplies. At the same time the enemies began to approach the walls step by step, discharging fire upon the city almost incessantly. The walls and everything inside them attract the enemies with a magnetic power, like the heart of the victim attracts the killer. Everybody

1   Croatian writer (1930).
2   Croatian writer from Dubrovnik (1857–1929).

Robert Leš / **Crafts of the ACY Marina, Dubrovačka rijeka, June 1992**

Milo Kovač / Shelling of the small island Lokrum — the forester's house, autumn 1991

Jadran Kapor (Dubrovački vjesnik) / Sustjepan in ruins,
Dubrovačka rijeka, February 10, 1992

Milo Kovač / Osojnik, a village near Dubrovnik, St. George's church, June 1992

Damir Fabijanić (Dubrovački vjesnik) / Sustjepan in Dubrovačka rijeka, June 1992

Božidar Đukić / **Destruction of the Hotel »Belvedere«, autumn 1991**

The ACY Marina, Dubrovačka rijeka, October 10, 1991

Robert Leš / **Mali Ston, June 1992**

Damir Fabijanić / Mali Ston, June 1992

Robert Leš / Slano, a small town 45 kilometres to the west of Dubrovnik, June 1992

Željko Šoletić / Slano, a small town 45 kilometres to the west of Dubrovnik, June 1992

Milo Kovač / Motif from Slano, June 1992

Damir Fabijanić / **Slano, June 1992**

Robert Leš / Brsečine, a village to the west of Dubrovnik, June 1992

Miljenko Mojaš / **Building outside the walls of Mali Ston, January 1992**

Miljenko Mojaš / Ston, residential building (ruins), January 1992

Miljenko Mojaš / **Destruction of Mali Ston, January 1992**

KATEGORIZACIJA OBJEKATA OŠTEĆENIH RATNIM
RAZARANJEM U MALOM STONU, prosinac 1991 g.

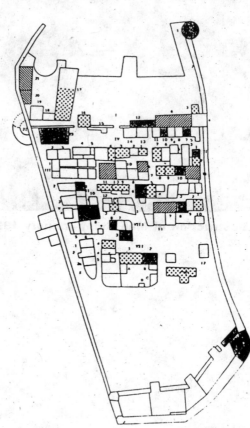

Categorization of buildings damaged by war actions against Mali Ston, December 1991

III KATEGORIJA (objekt sa oštećenom konstrukcijom zidova i krova)   IV KATEGORIJA (objekt sa rekonstruktivnim oštećenjima)

■ I. KATEGORIJA (potpuno izgoren objekt)   ▨ II KATEGORIJA (objekt sa oštećenom konstrukcijom zidova i krova)

Destroyed building with old mill on the Zvekovica, February 1992

Burnt–out house in Čilipi (Local history and memorial museum), February 1992

Burnt–out house in Čilipi, February 1992

The burnt–out village Močići (Konavle), February 1992

knows that the decisive role is given to the walls: "We shall shut ourselves into the old city and die if we must" said one of the leading men. At this point of the story, where reality can only be continued through a legend, comes the Saint, holding the City and its riddle.

Hecuba

If the Slave Girl[3] was one of the archetypes representing the fate of Croatia, today it is Hecuba. For several years I have known a woman who recently lost both sons and had to play Hecuba's role in real life. Her name is Katarina Liban and she comes from Mokošica[4]. And this is her lament directed towards the actors of the World's night which spread over Croatia:

"A group of young men, between 16 and 25 years of age, came out for a few minutes, from our air–raid shelter where, with hundreds of people, they had spent five days. Somebody, a traitor (or the Devil himself) gave a sign to the soldiers of the Yugoslav Army, who hovered on the hill above us like vultures. They kept us in this cage without food, water or medicine. The soldiers immediately began bombing. Nine young people were killed, and many more were wounded. Because of the onslaught of bombs and other projectiles that followed, we could not remove the bodies nor help the wounded. Blood flowed in streams and everything that I will ever see or hear in future will be blood, screams and tears."

"The Burnt Land"

Where there was a house, a corn–field, a wood, they already saw ruins, burnt land, ashes.

Where there was man, woman, child, they saw stains of blood. Dust and wind swept in their ears. Their eyes were already blinded, their ears already deafened, by the blaze, by the boom.

Where the sheep, cows, horses grazed, they saw carcasses.

Where they scented blood, they saw a spring, a stream, a river.

Where there was song, they already listened for a cry.

---

3   Title of a drama written by the Croatian writer Hanibal Lucić from Hvar (1485–1553).
4   A suburb west of Dubrovnik

Where there was a people, they opened the dark soil, already.

Observers

Some, arguing that they are not at war, are shooting at us: others observe it and swear they are impartial. Cold looks from one side and from the other: It is the symmetry that makes victims fall, fires burn, and destruction spread. Only by apparent disagreement between them could such a critical mass of evil come about. You will find it difficult to limit the evil, least of all by your blood stained discreetness: you will be taken into consideration.

"Macbeth" 1992

Raise your head and see how Burnham Forest

climbs the bared Mount of Srđ.[5]

The last inch

As the war draws near its end, the last inch keeps appearing in the foreground. The more unconsciously this small measure is used, the more landscape it holds. What an expanse of flattened lowland, crushed rubble, demolished wall: what a number of souls can stand on the last inch retreating with sound and fury.

Translated by Dora Maček

5   Hill overlooking the City of Dubrovnik.

Maren Frejdenberg

Dubrovnik's Destiny

The fury of the war in Yugoslavia has become aggravated: the federal army has begun to destroy the medieval parts of Dubrovnik from land and sea. This is senseless: Dubrovnik (in the olden times it was called Ragusa) is not a military base. The present attack has no precedent: no aggressor has ever tried to penetrate the city. Something else is amazing too: surrounded by ancient walls there stands the city — the undisputable master, fully preserving its historic shape.

Many valuable artefacts and famous architectural creations are concentrated in the city. One palace houses unique Archives to which there is no equal in Europe as to wealth, systematic arrangement and age. The Archives in Dubrovnik have been kept since the end of the 13th century. Historians, art historians and tourists from all over the world gather in Dubrovnik to admire them.

There is another important detail. One of the oldest synagogues in Europe is located in the very centre of the city; in the Žudioska ulica (i. e. the Jewish Street).

Is it possible to imagine what has moved the politicians and generals in Belgrade to commit themselves to such barbaric ways? It is not so much a question of longing for "military exploits", but an attempt to financially ruin Croatia, who has declared her independence from Yugoslavia. This becomes evident from the fact that the littoral, particularly Dubrovnik, has always brought a considerable sum of hard currency from the tourist trade to the state treasury. The latest events in Yugoslavia are evidence not only of the motives but also of the style cherished by politicians of a certain type. They are people who are capable to lift their hand against sacred cultural values of others in order to satisfy their own ambitions. Examples are Kremlj of 1918, the Temple of Christ the Saviour of 1935, and Dubrovnik of 1991.

("Vremja", Tel Aviv, October 11, 1991)

* * *

83

The world followed events in Dubrovnik for several months. The city became a kind of symbol of the tragic destiny of the Croatian nation. People from various countries learned about it and were at times compassionate with the Croats, or tried to understand who was right and who was wrong. Many did not know where the war was taking place. During these months Dubrovnik was destined to play a very important part, though a tragic one, of a landmark. I, who live in Israel, could see it happening.

Many with whom I talked would exclaim: "Look where Croatia lies! On the coast, where Dubrovnik is too." Others would say: "Of course, we spent a holiday in that wonderful city. How beautiful it is, how delicate! How can anyone shell it?" Finally, some (not many, but some nevertheless) would remark: "We heard that there is a synagogue built of timber, where exquisite Torah scrolls are kept. How can it be possible to want to destroy such treasure?"... The last reaction is particularly significant. I cannot speak in the name of the people of Israel, because I am an immigrant who has spent less than a year there. But what I can speak with certainty about is the deep respect of the people of Israel for all ancient monuments. Particularly those that relate to the past of the Jewish people. Among such monuments Dubrovnik occupies an important place.

On the top of the hill where the University of Tel–Aviv is situated there is a large Museum of the history of the dispersion of the Jewish people, a Museum of the diaspora. It is one of the most popular museums in the country with queues forming in front of its entrance every day. One of the exhibition halls contains models of famous synagogues from all over the world. When I looked at the model of the synagogue in Dubrovnik in June 1991, I felt it was an exceptional encounter.

Ten years ago, just as I had finished my book on Dubrovnik, entering the synagogue I met Emil Tolentino. He is a wise old man, who retained a keen intellect and wit.

— "Whose building is it?", I asked inadvertently, knowing that in "socialist" countries sacral buildings were usually expropriated by the state. — "What do you mean sir", exclaimed the old Jew. "What do you mean 'whose', the Jewish Community has been taking care of it for six hundred years!" And now, ten years after this encounter, after having looked at the exquisite collection and the building, I had to write the following words: "He (E. Tolentino) proudly showed me the Torah scrolls, saved from the Nazis during World War II, and told about the victims of the Jewish Community: only 9 people out of 146 were killed.

Could the old Jew have imagined that our treasures, preserved from the Nazis, would become a target for the weapons of the Yugoslav fleet?"

Besides, I am bound to the City with powerful ties. Twenty years ago led my scientific interest in the Middle Ages in Dalmatia to my acquaintance with the history of Dubrovnik. I spent several summers reading the published materials on this subject. Unfortunately it was only written material. As a Russian historian (at that time I lived in Kalinin, in the district of Tver on the Volga) I could not afford the "luxury" of visiting the City and working with its famous Archives. Besides, this was the lot of all other general historians — they were simply not allowed to travel abroad. The only way was to study written sources of information. I succeeded in acquiring the relevant literature, I acquired everything that was of interest to me. I am therefore indebted to the National and University Library, Library of the Croatian Academy of Arts and Sciences in Zagreb, and particularly to its Historical Institute in Dubrovnik. Now, when the country and Dubrovnik are experiencing such hard times, I wish to express my gratitude to these scientific institutions.

I am sure that I will be joined by those young researchers from the University of Kalinin (Tver), whose work with the materials about Dubrovnik has not only resulted in their doctoral theses (Irina Vorobeva, Natalija Lučinina, Evgenij Vecelj), but who have been my co–authors in the production of the book "Dubrovnik and the Ottoman Empire" ("Nauka", Moskva, 1984; second edition 1989).

It is possible that researchers who are acquainted with the Archives of Dubrovnik could find fault with our scientific treatment of the material, some of our conclusions may even meet with disagreement. But I firmly believe one thing. The picture of the development of the state of Dubrovnik, its mercantile and political activities, its everyday life that we presented in the book, fulfilled its role. It uncovered this splendid Croatian city and its unusual destiny to the Russian readers. Let this be our homage to the city.

(End of March, 1992)

* * *

Several weeks ago the war reports from Yugoslavia were full of information on Dubrovnik. Following the orders from Belgrade the Yugoslav Federal Army attacked the suburbs, and the naval artillery systematically bombarded the ancient towers, palaces and other monuments from the sea. Everything has calmed down now, the word Dubrovnik has disappeared from newspaper columns, and the mass exodus of the city's population seems to have ceased.

UNESCO commissions have begun assessing the extent of damage suffered by the city. It has been established, for instance, that the famous synagogue, present in the city ever since the 14th century, has been severely damaged — its windows and doors were broken, the roof demolished by two direct hits. The more important it is therefore to retrace the question: What has the Federal Army achieved by the attack on Dubrovnik? What did the government in Belgrade want from a totally unprotected city? The answer is simple enough, the beginning is to be found in the far away history, in the value attached to this city by all Southern Slavs. This value is to be found in the first place in the brilliant history of the city.

Indeed, it is very difficult to conceal the war in Dubrovnik. The conquest of Eastern Slavonia (the district around Vukovar, "Croatia's Stalingrad") could be justified as necessary for the protection of the local Serbian population, who were not granted autonomy by the present Croatian government in time. The intrusion into Krajina, the Dalmatian district around the town Knin, could hardly be justified on the same grounds. But the Serbian population of Dubrovnik makes now only about 6% of all its inhabitants. The siege of Dubrovnik, shelling it from the land and from the sea, a barbaric destruction of all the great values — fall into place in the deplorable list of evil deeds.

("Novosti" Tel Aviv, April 21, 1992)

* * *

Now as never before does the City need help of the international community and cooperation with. It seems to me that cooperation has to begin with the broadest international public becoming acquainted with the effects of war, with what has been destroyed and what has been preserved and in what condition. Information bulletins, pamphlets, brochures have to be sent all over the world.

The City has suffered a great deal during its long history always remaining an example of spiritual strength and endurance. If it succeeded in surviving the great earthquake of April 6, 1667 and endured what followed, it is an excellent example for those who now have to take up the cause of its revival.

---

*   The author is a Russian historian of Jewish origin. He has been studying the history of Dalmatia in the Middle Ages for over thirty years. He has published numerous texts on Croatian history including such as deal with Dubrovnik's past. The author is now researcher at the Diaspora Research Institute of the University of Tel Aviv.

Colin Kaiser

Dubrovnik: When the War is over

The Perfection of Old Dubrovnik

It is not a cliché to call Dubrovnik a jewel, for generally a jewel is small and finely worked. The image of Dubrovnik held in the hand of St. Blasius is equally fitting: the old town is a great city reduced in scale to human proportions. Its monuments are small, but given monumental proportions because of the effects of perspective (the cathedral seen from the column of Roland) or surprise (St. Blasius church seen as one arrives at the column of Roland or when one comes from the gate near the clock–tower). It is a marvel of continuity, beginning with the regulation of 1272, reinforced by the reconstructions following the earthquake of 1667 and the persistence of styles despite changing architectural and aesthetic fashions elsewhere in Europe. Through the effect of topography it balances between mountain and sea, and hovers between sea and sky like a bird. *The modesty of its people, symbolized by the rarity of its monuments to great men, and by the prevention of architectural extravagance designed to perpetuate the memory of a single man, mark it as a home for men of all social conditions.*

The duty of Dubrovnikers is to maintain this perfection by maintaining the authenticity of the old town.

The Different Facets of Authenticity

I ask the reader to consider the following opinion, given by the experts of the International Council on Monuments and Sites (ICOMOS) when confronted by the nomination request presented by the Yugoslavian government in 1978: "The ensemble of Dubrovnik is very characteristic of a situation where an excellent condition of presentation corresponds to a very serious loss of authenticity. This does not exclude favorable consideration for its inclusion (on the World Heritage List, note of the author)."

This opinion appears paradoxical until one considers that authenticity is composed of a number of elements. One is the architectural authenticity of stones. The experts drew up their opinion before a somewhat hasty restoration of the Palace of the Rectors, the "de–baroquisation" of the choir of the cathedral, the creation of the uncharacteristic, un–Dubrovnik exhibition space in the cinema complex, and the additions to the Primary and Music schools — the type of cultural intervention that could seriously damage the architectural authenticity of old Dubrovnik if repeated in the future. A second type of authenticity is the function of a building or an ensemble. It was this second element to which the experts were referring — in the case of old Dubrovnik, an economic function.

Dubrovnik did not have to experience an earthquake and the "Implementational Plan for the Historic Centre of Dubrovnik" that followed the earthquake in order to become an abscess of tourism. I mark my words carefully: it is not a question of being against tourism. When I was in Dubrovnik in November and December last year, people said to me that I must return after the war, "when the tourists come back". They were not just expressing a desire for a return to normal life. Tourism has become part of the way of life of Dubrovnik, indeed of the entire Dalmatian coast. It has entered into the character of a people, and it is indeed part of a tradition of hospitality. *The whole problem is one of measure.*

The experts of ICOMOS knew that Dubrovnik's entire existence and indeed identity was being centred around touristic development, as part of a national policy designed to earn foreign currency. It is interesting to leaf through publications on Dubrovnik that have a genuine cultural character: they never fail to boast of the number of hotels (outside of the old town), and in photographs of old Dubrovnik (always in the summer) the publishers always find a way of including artisan boutiques, a Stradun teaming with tourists, and crowded beaches with a view of St. John Fort and the small port. The beauty of old Dubrovnik under a grey winter sky is neglected, because there would be no tourists in the picture.

In a certain sense this kind of development was understandable. The Dalmatian coast has experienced a succession of economic crises in this century, from the phylloxera that sent many Croatians to the new world, the dislocation of the Adriatic economy that followed World War II, to the closing of shipyards in more recent times, which also led to emigration. The coast being what it is, simply beautiful, the Adriatic (on the Dalmatian side at least) being clean, there being a proliferation of fine old towns, country homes and monasteries, it is not surprising that former governments chose to put the accent on tourism. Hotels, some of discreet if *passe–partout* design, others concrete horrors, and boutiques mushroomed, as the government sought to meet all "Western" tastes.

A kind of monoculture was born, as in those African countries that grow peanuts or green beans for Western consumption — and which plunge into crisis when the international prices drop. Other countries which have undergone excessive tourist development have paid the price too, especially the Spanish and part of the French Mediterranean coast. People become tired of being massed on beaches and pushed into concrete boxes. They desert these kinds of places and take their holidays in countries or regions that have a less developed tourist infrastructure. The deserted regions become depressed areas — property values plunge, boutiques close, and people look for work elsewhere.

Tourists are not stupid: increasingly they value authenticity, and it is another kind of authenticity — not genuine handmade articles or buildings restored according to the canons of the Charter of Venice, but rather a *human authenticity*. They become tired of seeing other tourists and local people whose principal activity is trying to sell them something. And this is the crux of the problem: for an urban economy geared mainly to tourism eventually acquires only a service population of specialists: the others leave.

The Desire to Stay

In November and December 1991 in the course of my mission as UNESCO observer at Dubrovnik I visited many houses, a number of them in the Poljana Mrtvo Zvono, some of whose inhabitants had suffered severely in the war. Many, if not most of the people I saw and spoke with were what sociologists would describe as being of "modest social condition". Old Dubrovnik is their home and they have nowhere else to go. Above all, they do not wish to leave, whatever the very serious dangers they have to face. The war is not over, and no one can forget St. Nicholas Day. Yet one day it will end, and though Dubrovnik will have peace, *it will face other dangers*. For what war could not bring about — the mass evacuation of the old town — could happen through a type of urbanism that favours the massive development of tourism.

I referred to the Poljana Mrtvo Zvono, because I know that the entire southern third of the old town, including Pustijerna and the St. Mary Convent area, was to become a complex of tourist apartments and studios for artists, a centre for the arts and an archaeological museum, pizza parlours and night–clubs, and toilets for tourists. The people who live in the Poljana Mrtvo Zvono would have to go and live somewhere else. The "Implementational Town Plan for the Historic Centre of Dubrovnik" itself planned for the removal of 700 inhabitants of Dubrovnik out of the 4, 200 people recorded on the 1981 census. In 1978, according to the nomination file for the World Heritage list presented by the Yugoslavian government, Dubrovnik had 5, 255 inhabitants, which meant — if this information is correct — that the old town was steadily losing inhabitants. In other words, while a certain attention was being given to the stones of Dubrovnik — a major attraction for foreign tourists — little was foreseen to prevent *homo dubrovnikus* from becoming a rare species. And it is *homo dubrovnikus*, modest, kind and courageous, who is the real treasure of Dubrovnik.

After the War

We all know from the information provided by the Croatian government, but also by Western journalists and the various missions of international and regional organisations, that the Croatian economy has been greviously damaged by the war. While a certain amount of international financial aid can be expected in the form of credits for exportation, low interest loans, joint ventures, it will be unwise to count too much upon Western Europe and the United States, which have their own problems, and which are continuously being solicited by Eastern European countries and the various ex–Soviet states. Inasmuch as the Dalmatian coast and especially Dubrovnik are concerned the temptation will be to return to a tourist economy because, to a certain degree, that worked. The temptation will be to return to the "Implementational Plan" for Dubrovnik. But those Western Europeans seeking human authenticity will be discouraged from coming and the generalized economic crisis will prevent others from coming. A new chapter in the book of crises for the Dalmatian coast and Dubrovnik will be opened, and the principal victim will be the people of the region.

The people of old Dubrovnik will be especially exposed. On the one hand a concentration of investment in the more important buildings will simply permit many houses to deteriorate still further, and this will ultimately drive many citizens out of the old town. On the other, in the context of the privatization of property and restoration and rehabilitation of houses some people will have to leave the old town for other reasons. How will they be able to pay for the restoration and rehabilitation of the houses they live in, but which they have difficulties in claiming title to? This could well be one of the worst consequences of continuing former urban policy. A way must be found to permit the inhabitants of the old town to become the owners of their houses, or at least permit them to have long–term leases.

This analysis — this warning — is a personal one. It is not a criticism of those local people who carried out past planning measures: the political and economic contexts were different and those contexts imposed particular constraints. All the actors in Dubrovnik will have to work together, architects, engineers, planners, economists, the municipality, the people — who must become actors in development and not be passive spectators.

The future of old Dubrovnik cannot be decided in isolation of the future of the whole town. Ploče and Pile cannot simply turn into "filters" for tourist traffic and accordingly sacrificed to the old town: they too have a right to live. The future of Dubrovnik must be planned in the context of the whole region: this is the meaning of "integrated conservation". While tourism will remain an important element in the economy, that economy must be diversified and largely re–oriented towards the Adriatic and Mediterranean world, which made Dubrovnik what it is.

Cultural Heritage and Human Heritage

In the forums of culture people talk a lot about heritage and man, and these discourses remain abstract and disconnected from daily life. In this cruel war the discourse has come down to earth. For me it was written in the faces of Dubrovnikers. The stones of Dubrovnik also took on a particular meaning — the walls of the old town and the narrow streets that provided protection to human flesh, the old cisterns that could be filled with water, the thick stone walls of houses that refused to collapse in one big bombardment (but could collapse under a new rain of mortars, rockets and perhaps howitzer shells). The old town reasserted its function as protector of people. But it protects people who wish to remain in it. Dubrovnik is first and foremost a home for its people. It may be on the World Heritage List, and therefore a treasure for humanity, but its sun, sky and stones have permitted the virtues of *homo dubrovnikus* to flourish down through the centuries. Your duty is not just to stones, but to stones and this man.

(Colin Kaiser is by training a social and institutional historian of Old Regime Europe and was Director of the International Council on Monuments and Sites /ICOMOS/ from 1987 to 1991. The opinions he expresses in this article are his own and he does not speak on behalf of UNESCO.)

Bruno Carnez

QUI T'A PERMIS D'ETRE
AUSSI BELLE?

À Dubrovnik

Qui t'a permis d'être aussi belle?
Jamais tu m'as semblé si belle;
Pourquoi les plus belles fleurs sont celles,
Qui dorment seules au fond du ciel.

Tes yeux verts pleurent un rêve doux
Laissant couler une larme de diamant;
Ton sourire est un gris velours,
Une caresse parmi l'enfer du temps.

Quand ces yeux pourtant se font flammes,
L'espoir s'enfuit, vaincu par le ciel noir;
C'est ton rire, tel celui de Diane,
Qui me pourchasse dans les brouillards du soir.

Mille reflets éclairent tes cheveux,
Comme un soleil sur les vagues argentées;
Ton profil, relief mélodieux,
Est symphonie d'un rêve inavoué.

Ton image ne pourra s'enfuir
Loin du chaos, abîme de mes pensées;
Ton visage est un élixir,
Fidèle onguent pour un coeur blessé.

4 avril 1992.

Chronology of the Wartime Events

The Start of the War in Konavle and Župa dubrovačka

During September, the so–called Yugoslav Army occupies border territory towards Konavle and Župa dubrovačka. On September 17, 1991, a panel discussion is held by the Croatian Cultural Organization, Matica Hrvatska, in Dubrovnik on Greater Serbian expansionism as related to Dubrovnik; a naval blockade of Dubrovnik begins. The Army pulls out of the artillery battery positioned at Cape Goli on Mljet. Dubrovnik is put on air–raid alert at around midnight. The Yugoslav Army steps up the deployment of forces along the border near Dubrovnik. On the night of September 23, 1991, Vitaljina comes under fire for the first time and 144 residents are evacuated. Brgat is targeted from Ivanica. On September 25, Vitaljina and Brgat are attacked once again and enemy warships group around Molunat. On September 26, attacks on Konavle and Župa dubrovačka intensify. Vitaljina is abandoned. The number of refugees from Konavle and Župa dubrovačka grows (around 466). On September 27, European observers arrive in Dubrovnik.

September 30, 1991 — December 31, 1991

Monday, September 30

— At 5 p. m., the Command of the Boka Naval Sector announces a naval blockade of Dubrovnik coastal waters.

Tuesday, October 1

— At 6 a. m., the eastern part of the municipality is attacked with all available weaponry. At 6.10 a. m., Župa dubrovačka and Rijeka dubrovačka are targeted. Electricity is cut off in the regions of Konavle, Župa dubrovačka, Rijeka dubrovačka, and along the Dubrovnik coast down to Slano as well as the town of Dubrovnik itself. Two airplanes fire rockets at the transmitter and relay station on Mt. Srđ which leaves Dubrovnik without telephone lines. Radio links with other parts of Croatia and the world are weakened considerably. Nor is the island of Lokrum spared. Slano comes under artillery fire which prevents the passenger boat, Perast, from sailing out of the harbour. Parish churches are also damaged: St. Blaze in Pridvorje together with a Franciscan monastery, the Holy Trinity in Gruda, St. Mary Magdelene in Mandaljena, St. Ann in Brgat, The Chapel of the Annunciation at the approach to Rijeka dubrovačka, and the Parish Church of St. George on Osojnik.

— Dubrovnik is under complete blockade, without electricity, water and telephone lines. HAM radio operators become the only link with the outside world.

— Classes in schools are suspended.

— Head of the EC monitor mission, Martin Berthould, states that they were shocked by what they had experienced. Even more so because they spoke the day before with representatives of the Federal army and there had been no sign that Dubrovnik was under any threat.

Wednesday, October 2

— Fierce fighting is waged on Osojnik and in Čepikuće. Mokošica comes under machine gun fire from land and sea. The ship yard in Mokošica is leveled. The Church of the Holy Spirit in Komolac and St. Stephen's in Sustjepan are damaged during a bombardment. During the night, the most brutal battles are waged in Konavle along the entire border towards Prevlaka, Debeli brijeg, Dubravka, and Dunave as well as the areas bordering Herzegovina near Ivanjica and along the entire Dubrovnik coastline.

Thursday, October 3

— Thousands of hectares of forest are burning in the regions of Konavle, Župa, Brgat, Rijeka dubrovačka, Slano and Čepikuće. The famous ARBORETUM in Trsteno is also in flames.

Saturday, October 5

— The enemy reaches as far as Radovčići in Konavle. On the western battlefront, the enemy uses tanks in their advance on Slano. At 6 p. m., a gunboat opens fire on Ploče and the suburbs of Dubrovnik.

— The writer, Milan Milišić, is killed in his apartment during the attack on Ploče.

— The first "war–time edition" of Dubrovnik's daily paper is printed and distributed free of charge.

— The Church of St. Ann in Brsečine is damaged.

Sunday, October 6

— Enemy aircraft once again fire rockets at the transmitter on Mt. Srđ.

— The Dubrovnik airport is bombarded. Slano is targeted by artillery fire and fierce battles are waged near Osojnik.

Monday, October 7

— The enemy manages to break through to Cavtat but do not succeed in taking it. The local church and monastery in Cavtat is hit. Croatian defense forces repel advances on Ivanjica and Osojnik.

Tuesday, October 8

— Heavy guns pound Cavtat and the "Croatia" hotel.

Thursday, October 10

— Radio Dubrovnik begins to broadcast each hour from 6.30 to 20.30.
— A fierce battle is waged on Zvekovica.

Friday, October 11

— Head of the Crisis Coordination Centre Željko Šikić, mayor Pero Poljanić and a member of the executive council, Hrvoje Macan meet with the commander of the Boka Naval Sector, Admiral Miodrag Jokić. The meeting is held in the presence of EC monitors on the destroyer "Kotor" in the waters off Molunat. A ceasefire is agreed to and a meeting is scheduled for the next day near the Čilipi airport but is never held.

Saturday, October 12

— The blockade of the Dubrovnik port is lifted at 12. 30 p. m.

Sunday, October 13

— Houses are looted and torched in Konavle.
— All transportable equipment and supplies are taken out of Čilipi airport.
— Nikša (Čićo) Obuljen, Đuro Kolić and Hrvoje Macan are chosen to negotiate with the Yugoslav Army. Talks resume in Močići in the presence of EC observers.

Monday, October 14

— Members of the EC monitor mission continue talks with the Yugoslav Army without the presence of representatives from the Dubrovnik municipality.

Tuesday, October 15

— After talks in Močići near the Dubrovnik airport, the aggressor army enters Cavtat with the EC monitor mission and representatives of the Dubrovnik municipal assembly looking on.

Thursday, October 17

— A fresh enemy offensive commences on all fronts in the Dubrovnik region. Houses are destroyed and torched along the coast. Fierce battles rage in Župa dubrovačka and west of the Mokošica–Pobrežje line.

Friday, October 18

— Stara and Nova Mokošica, Komolac, Sustjepan, Brgat, Kupari, Gruž and Ploče are pounded from air, sea and land.

Saturday, October 19

— Despite the Hague ceasefire, Rijeka dubrovačka and Župa dubrovačka are rocked by mortar fire once again.
— Members of the Cavtat Crisis Coordination Centre are arrested by the Yugoslav Army.
— Some 3500 refugees being put up in the "Dubrava–Babin Kuk" hotel and tourist centre lack food and water.

Sunday, October 20

— Fighting rages on all fronts.
— The church of St. Mary Magdelene is hit in the village of Mandaljena in Župa dubrovačka.

Monday, October 21

— Backed by tanks, enemy forces manage to cross the barricades in Duboka Ljuta and reach the Kostur Solina line near Mlini in Župa dubrovačka.

Tuesday, October 22

— A fresh artillery attack on Župa dubrovačka commences early in the morning with Kupari and Srebreno especially hard hit.
— EC observers leave Dubrovnik saying that they are tired of trying so hard to establish contact between the two sides and normalize life in this region.
— A brutal attack from land and sea commences at dusk on Lapad. Hotels accomodating refugees are hit — the "Tirena", "Minčeta", "Dubrovnik–Palace" and "Park". The maternity ward in the Medarevo hospital is hit. A large number of civilian targets are damaged.

Wednesday, October 23

— Apart from the city regions: Lapad, Gruž, Ilijina glavica, Dance and Ploče, shells fired from land and sea pound the very heart of the city: Stradun, the house where Ruđer Bošković was born, the Sponza Palace, the Rupe Museum and the Synagogue.

Božidar Đukić / Čepikuće, June 1992

Božidar Đukić / **Lisac, June 1992**

Božidar Đukić / Mlini–Trgovište, July 1992

Milo Kovač / Airport — Čilipi, November 1992

Božidar Đukić / Ivan Meštrović: Mausoleum Račić, Cavtat — photo,
September 1993

Božidar Đukić / **Franciscan Monastery, Pridvorje — photo,
September 1993**

Mato Rilović / Gruda — photo, February 1993

Mato Rilović / Čilipi — photo, September 13, 1993

Thursday, October 24

— An amphibious landing is carried out on Kupari. Dubrovnik and its suburbs are bombarded. The Church of St. Jacob, the Benedictine Monastery of St. Jacob, and the Church of St. Dominic are all damaged.

Friday, October 25

— Following the landing on Kupari, defense forces withdraw from Župa dubrovačka and Brgat.

— EC monitor mission negotiations are held in Cavtat between representatives of Dubrovnik authorities and the Yugoslav Army. An order for a ceasefire is issued at 5 p. m. by the Boka Naval Sector Command.

Saturday, October 26

— The ferry, Slavija, manages to enter the Gruž harbour after three unsuccessful attempts.

Sunday, October 27

— Dubrovnik, Ston and the Ston coastal region are bombarded. The Sorkočević Renaissance palace in Rijeka dubrovačka is also fired upon.

— The EC demands that the Yugoslav Army abide by the ceasefire agreed to on October 18 and to lift its siege of Dubrovnik as well as to allow for the delivery of medical supplies and equipment to the city. At the same time, the request from the Yugoslav Army that the Croatian police surrender their arms is condemned with the explanation that this would mean the surrendering of the city.

Monday, October 28

— The Yugoslav Army takes Žarkovica while EC observers and representatives of the Dubrovnik municipal council are on route to talks in Cavtat. On the western battlefront, the enemy manages to reach as far as Mokošica.

— Daniel Janicot, head of Federico Mayor's office (UNESCO), arrives in Dubrovnik.

— News conferences are held regularly.

— The Libertas convoy sets off from Zagreb.

Tuesday, October 29

— At 1 p. m., the ambassadors of Italy, Great Britain, Holland and Greece (Sergio Vento, Peter E. Hall, Johanes Fietaars and Eleftherios) sail into the Old Town port together with the US deputy ambassador, Robert Rackmales, and military attachés from Italy, Great Britain, Greece and the United States. Hrvoje Kačić, the chairman of the Croatian Parliamentary Committee for Foreign Policy, accompanies them and they stay in Dubrovnik for around two hours. Both they and reporters are prohibited from travelling by land.

Wednesday, October 30

— The ship Balkanija arrives in the morning in Dubrovnik with some eighty tons of aid sent by the Bosnian Red Cross.

Thursday, October 31

— After being stopped several times by the Yugoslav Army, the Libertas flotilla sails into Gruž harbour shortly after 6 a. m. Some 800 people are on board the Slavija and 29 other vessels. Among them are President of the Federal Presidency Stipe Mesić, Croatian Prime Minister Franjo Gregurić, Croatian Parliamentary Vice–President Stjepan Sulimanac, Croatian Deputy Prime Minister Milan Ramljak, as well as many prominent public figures. After mass in the Dubrovnik Cathedral, a gathering is held in front of the Church of St. Blaze.

Friday, November 1

— A several hour long bombardment commences at 5 p. m. from both land and sea. The city regions of Gruž, Kantafig, Lapad and Montovjerna are attacked.

Saturday, November 2

— From 4 p. m., the entire city region, in particular Gruž and Lapad, is subjected to a fierce land and sea attack with all available weaponry.

Sunday, November 3

— Fifteen teams of journalists (BBC, ITN, Daily Telegraph, Reuter, France Press, Sky News, etc.) are covering the destruction of Dubrovnik.

Monday, November 4

— Dubrovnik and the nearby islands of Koločep and Šipan are bombarded.

Wednesday, November 6

— Dubrovnik suffers its fiercest attack so far. It is conducted from land and sea. A major attack is mounted from Žarkovica on Mt. Srđ and Bosanka where units of the Croatian Army are positioned. Shells fall on all parts of the city. The Jewish and Catholic Cemeteries are both hit. The 11th Century Benedictine Monastery on Lokrum is targeted by a gunboat.

— From the start of aggression on October 28, 52 people were killed and 202 were wounded in Dubrovnik, while 259 people were taken prisoner and more than 15,000 were displaced from their homes.

Thursday, November 7

— Fierce fighting is reported around Slano.

Friday, November 8

— The first issue of "Glas iz Dubrovnika" (The Voice from Dubrovnik) is printed in both Croatian and English.

— Fierce attacks are carried out on Bosanka and the Imperial Fort on Mt. Srđ.

Saturday, November 9

— Attacks on Gruž and Lapad are reported. Gunboats open fire indiscriminately. Many boats and ships are set ablaze and sunk in Gruž harbour, among them the "Argolys" and the "Delta" tugboat. Also hit are the hotels "Dubrovnik Palace", "Tirena", "Argentina", "Belvedere", and "Libertas." Shells hit the Bishop's Palace, the Capucine Monastery of Our Mother of Mercy, the Church of St. Vincent de Paul in Pile, The Church of the Holy Cross in Gruž, The Church of St. Blaze in Gorica, The Church of Our Mother of Mercy and the Convent of the Sisters of Mercy in Pile.

Sunday, November 10

— Artillery attacks resume in the early morning hours on the entire city especially on Lapad and Gruž. The Hotel Belvedere is systematically targeted from a gunboat and is set ablaze. Also hit are the Dominican Monastery of the Holy Cross in Gruž dating from 1437, the Sigurate Monastery dating from the 11th Century within the walls of the old town, and the Izvijačica Convent. The Minčeta fort is also hit. A large number of apartment complexes are destroyed.

— The Hotel Argentina where EC observers and foreign reporters are staying is attacked.

— Fifteen people are killed and 32 wounded.

— The first edition of the children's paper, "Glasić iz Dubrovnika" (The Tiny Voice from Dubrovnik) is printed.

Monday, November 11

— Attacks on all parts of the town begin at 6. 10 a. m., under the order, as reported by HAM Radio operators, to target everything that moves. The following structures and sites are hit: Minčeta Fort, St. John's Fort, the Old Town port, the Cathedral, Rector's Palace, Rupe Museum, the Jesuit Church, the Church of St. Jacob in Višnjica, the Church of our Savior dating from 1521, the church in Boninovo, St. Dominic's Monastery, the Franciscan Monastery dating from 1371, the Benedictine Monastery of St. Jacob, and the Dominican Monastery of the Holy Cross in Gruž dating from 1437. Hotels in Babin Kuk are also damaged, and shells penetrate bomb shelters packed with refugees. Three people are killed and many injured. The Hotels "Excelsior", "Argentina", "Tirena", and "Imperial" are also hit. Hundreds of boats are in flames in the Gruž harbour. A gunboat targets Lokrum.

— Drinking water is available only in hospitals and bakeries.

— The EC monitor mission in Zagreb called for an evacuation of its members from Dubrovnik. Three monitors state that they wanted to remain there and volunteered to share in the suffering of the citizens of Dubrovnik.

Tuesday, November 12

— A fresh artillery attack on the Imperial Fort commences at 6. 20 a. m. Shells fall on the town port, on Lovrijenac, St. John's fortress, Stradun, the Sponza Palace, Prijeko, and the Bell Tower. The first hit are Gruž, Lapad, Montovjerna, Pile, Ploče, Mokošica, and Rijeka dubrovačka. Once again, hotels in Babin Kuk, then "Excelsior", "Argentina", and "Imperial", are targeted. The Orlando Bakery is also shelled. All of Gruž harbour is in flames. Several shells also strike the hospital in Medarevo. The following churches are damaged: St. Jacob's in Višnjica, St. Ignatius, St. Dominic's, the Holy Cross in Gruž, St. Mihovil in Lapad, a new church on Mihajlo, the Church of St. Andrew's in Pile and the monasteries: the Dominican, the St. Jacob Benedictine, of Baby Jesus in Gospino polje, of the Daughters of the Salvation of God's Love in Lapad, and the Franciscan in Rožat.

— Croatian defense forces retreat from Komolac.

Wednesday, November 13

— Artillery attacks on the town continue.

Thursday, November 14

— A general alert remains in effect for the fifth day in a row.

— Rain begins to fall and people come out from their shelters to collect the rain water for drinking and hygiene purposes.

— The boat Slavija sails out of Dubrovnik carrying some 4000 women, children, sick and elderly.

Friday, November 15

— The all clear is sounded at 6.30 a. m. bringing an end to a general alert which had been in effect since November 9 at 7.26 a. m.

— The hydrofoil "Krila Dubrovnika" (The Wings of Dubrovnik) sailing under the UNICEF flag brings to Dubrovnik Michel Bonnot and Steffan de Mistura, UNICEF officials from Paris, as well as French Welfare Minister Bernard Kouchner, Italian Immigration Minister Margherita Boniver, and the military attaché from the French Embassy in Belgrade, Jacques Delaiques. The group has come to Dubrovnik to get a first hand look at the situation.

Sunday, November 17

— After Italian President Cossiga intervened several times, Yugoslav federal authorities finally allow the Italian boat San Marco to sail into Dubrovnik in order to deliver medicine and food.

Margherita Boniver: "It is completely unbelievable that such things can be happening somewhere that is only an hour flight from Rome. I'm furious at the indifference by which the world is observing the events here."

Bernard Kouchner: "I'm doing everything I can to inform the world about the plight of Vukovar and Dubrovnik, as well as all of Croatia, and I'm seeking help because I'm astounded by what I've experienced."

Monday, November 18

— At 12. 30 p. m., the San Marco carrying relief aid from Italy sails into Gruž harbour thus opening a humanitarian aid corridor. As the ship enters the port, enemy forces occupy Stara Mokošica and begin to plunder it.

Tuesday, November 19

— The Italian ship San Marco which sailed from Dubrovnik last night arrives in Brindisi with 782 refugees on board (women, children and elderly).

Wednesday, November 20

— The French hospital ship "La Rance" sails into Gruž harbour with relief aid in the form of medicines and medical supplies.

Thursday, November 21

— The third foreign vessel sailing under the UNICEF flag, the Rhodos II, enters Gruž harbour carrying medicine and food. Representatives of the International Red Cross from Geneva are on board.

— The Yugoslav Army enters Nova Mokošica.

Friday, November 22

— The French hospital ship "La Rance" sets sail from Gruž harbour in the morning with 300 mothers, children and the sick on board.

— The torching and looting of homes in Komolac and Stara Mokošica continue.

— Croatian defense forces manage to hold on to Čepikuće.

— Bernard Kouchner calls on world figures to come to the town which he describes as the heritage of the world.

Saturday, November 23

— Liburnija sets sail for Zelenika with 1600 passengers on board.

Sunday, November 24

— Escorted by the Italian warship Euro, the Italian tanker Simeto arrives in Dubrovnik carrying 1100 tons of drinking water under an arrangement organized by UNICEF.

— Under the patronage of the occupying army, a meeting is held in Cavtat of "the Movement for the Autonomy of the Dubrovnik Republic" led by Aco Apolonije, who was the district attorney under communism in Dubrovnik without any support from the population.

Monday, November 25

— The Maltese ship Dimaratos, with humanitarian aid from the International Committee of the Red Cross, sails into Gruž harbour.

— An air attack occurs on Ston.

Tuesday, November 26

— The Italian ship Paladio also arrives carrying a substantial amount of food, water and medicine.

— The firing of rockets on Ston continues. In attacks yesterday and today, the very centre of the town, the city walls and the Stoviš fort are damaged.

Wednesday, November 27

— The hydrofoil, "Krila Dubrovnika" sailing under the UN flag, arrives with special envoys for UNESCO's general director, Colin Kaiser and Bruno Carnez, on board. During their stay, they collect information concerning the damage sustained by cultural monuments.

— The ship Paladio evacuates 900 residents from Dubrovnik when it sets sail from the town in the morning.

— The Municipal Crisis Coordination Centre bans residents from leaving the city except in exceptional cases.

Thursday, November 28

— The ferry Liburnija arrives with more aid sent by, among others, the Bosnian Red Cross.

— Rodos II sails into Sobra on Mljet with humanitarian aid and medicine organized by the International Committee of the Red Cross in Geneva. This marks the end of the two month siege of the island.

Friday, November 29

— Bernard Kouchner, French Welfare Minister, returns to Dubrovnik. He is accompanied by Jean d'Ormesson, a member of the French Academy, and co–owner of the paper "Le Figaro" as well as by André Glucksmann, a well–

known French author and philosopher, and Jean Marie Caro and Charles Pistre, two academicians.

Sunday, December 1

— Organized by the Libertas flotilla and under the auspices of French Welfare Minister Bernard Kouchner, the Festival of Peace — the Truth about the City begins. An Intellectual Forum is held and convened by Dr. Slobodan Lang and his guests are Jean d'Ormesson and André Glucksmann.

— "La Rance", the French hospital ship sails into Gruž harbour delivering a large quantity of food and medicine.

— The Yugoslav Navy uses the arrival of "La Rance" to enter the port of Zaton.

Tuesday, December 3

— Rhodos II sails in with a relief shipment.

Thursday, December 5

— A concert "Mozart from Dubrovnik to the World" is held at the Music School.

— Fierce fighting is waged east of Ston.

Friday, December 6 (St. Nicholas' Day)

— The fiercest attack so far is carried out on the area within the ancient town walls. It begins at 5.50 a. m. with a fierce artillery, tank and mortar barrage on Imperial Fortress on Mt. Srđ, and it spreads to the city which is put on general alert at 7.15 a. m. Yugoslav Naval gunboats join in the attack. The destruction is immense. Fires rage throughout the town. Firefighters are killed when trying to extinguish them.

— Some six hundred shells strike the historic old town centre.

— A total of 19 people are killed and more than sixty are seriously wounded.

— Cyrus Vance sends a note of protest to General Kadijević.

— Italian Immigration Minister Margherita Boniver issues an appeal to save Dubrovnik after a dramatic plea was made from Dubrovnik by Steffan de Mistura, UNICEF's representative.

— Numerous buildings are damaged, among them: The Sponza Palace, the Church of St. Blaze, the Cathedral, the Franciscan Monastery, the Dominican Monastery, the Rector's Palace... (see other documents on this). Hardly any building is spared.

— The Inter–University Centre is burned to the ground together with the library which had a 25,000 book collection.

— The cross on Mt. Srđ is also destroyed.

— The headquarters of the Dubrovnik Festival together with documentation collected over 43 years went up in flames.

Saturday, December 7

— An agreement is reached during talks in Srebreno on a complete cessation of hostilities, the lifting of the blockade of Gruž harbor and the opening of sea traffic from Cavtat, Lopud, Šipan and Mljet. The Croatian side at the negotiations is represented by Davorin Rudolf, Ivan Cifrić, and Petar Kriste while Vice–Admiral Miodrag Jokić represents the Yugoslav Army.

Sunday, December 8

— The "Cap d'Afrique" is finally allowed to enter Gruž harbour after being stopped by the Yugoslav Army for four days. The "La Rance" is sailing with it.

Tuesday, December 10

— After 70 days under naval blockade, sea traffic between Mljet and the mainland is restored.

Thursday, December 12

— The Libertas II flotilla sails into Gruž harbour.

Friday, December 13

— 135 civilians and Croatian Army troops who had spent 72 days imprisoned in Morinje, Trebinje, and Bileća are released. They are taken to Split on the boat "Rhodos".

— The ferry "Slavija" brings in members of the Croatian Academy of Arts and Sciences, of the Croatian cultural organization Matica Hrvatska, of the St. Blaze Fund, the Academy of Theater Arts and of the Croatian Parliament as well as others who are to participate in the "Conference on the Town and Municipality of Dubrovnik — its renewal and future development."

— Sea traffic between Dubrovnik and Cavtat is restored but only for vessels carrying humanitarian relief aid.

— Fierce attacks are reported in the Ston region.

Saturday, December 14

— A Conference on the renewal and future development of Dubrovnik is held in the "Luka Sorkočević" Music School under the sponsorship of the Croatian Academy of Arts and Sciences. Participating are members of the Academy and from the University of Croatia, Matica Hrvatska, the Croatian P.E.N. Centre, and the Croatian Writers' Society.

Thursday, December 19

— Peter Galbraith, a high ranking advisor to the United States Senate committee for foreign relations, and James Rubin, a member of the United States Senate subcommittee for Europe, travel to Dubrovnik at the request of a special Senate commission with the aim of investigating what the overall situation is in former Yugoslavia.

Saturday, December 21

— A relief convoy from the Bosnian capital of Sarajevo arrives on the ferry "Ilirija."

Sunday, December 22

— "A Tribute to Silvije Strahimir Kranjčević" (a Croatian writer) is held in the Franciscan Church. The actors Niko Kovač and Ivo Dragojević take part as well as Cappella Ragusina, Linđo, the soloists Srđan Berdović, Vesna Miletić–Corona, Mladen Glavinović, and Tamara Glavinović–Opalić. Lyrics were put to music by Krešimir Magdić.

Tuesday, December 24 (Christmas Eve)

— For security reasons, there is no midnight mass held anywhere in the city area.

Wednesday, December 25 (Christmas)

— Thanks to the tremendous efforts of workers from the Dubrovnik division of the Croatian power company and from the Split–based companies "Elektroprijenos" and "Elektroprivreda", electricity is restored to some parts of the city for the first time in 86 days.

Thursday, December 26

— A Christmas Concert conducted by Đelo Jusić is held in the Franciscan Church. Taking part are the Festival Orchestra, the "Libertas" Choir, and the Dubrovnik children's choir group.

Friday, December 27

— There is still no water in the city.

Saturday, December 28

— Some parts of the city receive water after 89 days without it.
— A delegation from the University of Zagreb, led by its dean, Dr. Marijan Šunjić, arrives. An agreement on the reconstruction of the Inter–University Center is signed as well.

Sunday, December 29

— At 11 p. m., a radio message is received from the Boka Naval Sector Command which announces a ban on vessels sailing into or out of Gruž harbour.

Monday, December 30

— After the unexplained ban announced by the Yugoslav Army, it nevertheless allowed the ferry "Liburnija" to leave the port and it brought back performers for the "Concert of Peace" from Bari.

Tuesday, December 31

— "The Concert of Peace" is held at midnight in the Franciscan Church. Taking part are the National Orchestra from Toulouse and soloists Barbara Hendricks, soprano and the violist, Jean Stanienda. The Dubrovnik childrens' choir also participated. J. S. Bach and Mozart were performed. Along with numerous guests, the concert was attended by Croatian Parliamentary President Žarko Domljan, French Minister Bernard Kouchner, and UN Secretary General envoy and UNICEF representative Steffan de Mistura, Tedjini Hadam, head of the synagogue in Paris, and Peter Brook and Michel Piccoli. A number of TV networks throughout Europe and the world broadcast the event live.

Compiled by Nora Cervelin

From the beginning of January till 25 May 1992 the city area of Dubrovnik was surrounded by the enemy army while a significant part of the territory of Dubrovnik Commune was occupied. During those months the defenders of the Town resisted courageously to continuous provocations of Serbian and Montenegrin soldiery. Although bursts of fire were incessantly directed towards various city areas, a direct and consistent artillery attack on Dubrovnik did not occur at that time.

Monday, May 25

— The Yugoslav Army withdrew from the western part of the Commune.
— Slano was freed. Leaving the place the occupiers have stolen several paintings from St. Jerom's convent.
— The Yugoslav Navy has completely left the Island of Mljet.

Tuesday, May 26

— The Yugoslav Army left the western part of the Commune: Mokošica, Žarkovica, Dubac, Strinčjera and Bosanka.

Wednesday, May 27

— The Yugoslav army was repulsed from the southeastern part of the Commune, from the region of Župa dubrovačka to the area of Plat.

* * *

Eighteen days under continuous alarm. From their positions in the Commune of Trebinje (The Republic of Bosnia and Hercegovina) and from their positions in the occupied region of Konavle, the enemy mainly attacked with heavy artillery the region of Župa dubrovačka, city area, even the City itself, and Rijeka dubrovačka.

Those attacks continued even after that, until 20 July 1992.

Friday, May 29

— The following buildings are hit in today's attacks: The Church of St. Blaze, Rector's Palace, the Little Fountain in Gundulić's field, the St. Clare Convent, the National Library, the Franciscan Monastery, the Serbian Orthodox Church, the Cathedral, the Minčeta Fort, and palaces on Getaldić and Božidarević Streets.

Saturday, May 30

— An enemy gunboat is destroyed.

— The Dubrovnik Medical Centre is given a 200–bed mobile hospital with equipment from the Danish town of Roskilde.

Sunday, May 31

— The Yugoslav Navy pulls out from Lastovo.

Monday, June 1

— Following a two day stay, Hans Staudinger, an official with the United Nations High Commissioner for Refugees, leaves. He delivered 27 tons of food for the 23,600 refugees and displaced persons in the Dubrovnik municipality.

— The following buildings or sites are damaged in today's attacks: the large Onofrio's Fountain, the Bokar Fortress, the St. Mary quarter, and the Rupe Museum.

Friday, June 5

— Dubrovnik remains without electricity and as of today, water will be available every other day in different parts of town.

Monday, June 8

— The following buildings or sites are hit in today's attacks: The Franciscan Monastery, the Dominican Monastery, the town's Bell Tower, the Rupe Museum, the palaces within the Old Town, the building housing the Institute for Reconstruction, the Sponza Palace which houses the Archives, the Skočibuha Palace together with the Science Library.

Thursday, June 11

— It takes 17 days for relief aid to reach Cavtat for the residents of Konavle and Cavtat. The boat "Astral" delivered the humanitarian assistance and it later returned at irregular intervals.

Friday, June 19

— An enemy ship is hit and incapacitated.

— The following buildings and sites are damaged: the Franciscan Church, the Dominican Monastery, the Sponza Palace, the Synagogue, the Music School, the Orthodox Church, the Mosque, the Rupe Museum, the Church of St. Joseph, palaces in the Old Town, the Cathedral, the Church of St. Blaze, the Rendić fountain in Pile, and the Bokar Fortress.

Thursday, June 25

— This is the 22nd day without electricity.

Monday, June 29

— The following buildings and sites are damaged: the Franciscan Monastery, the Convent of the Sisters of Service and Mercy, the Bishopric, the Minčeta Fortress, the forts of Lovrjenac and Revelin, the towers of St. Catherine, St. Frances and St. Barbara, the walls around the Old Town (in several places), and residential buildings both within and outside of the walls.

Wednesday, July 1

— In today's attacks the following buildings or sites are damaged: the Minčeta Fortress, the forts of Lovrjenac and Revelin, the towers of St. Catherine, St. Frances and St. Barbara, and the Old Town walls.

Friday, July 3rd

— This is the 31st day without electricity.

Thursday, July 9

— Deputy Commander of the EC monitor mission, British general David Cranston, visits Dubrovnik.

Friday, July 10

— This is the 37th day without electricity.

— The 43rd Dubrovnik Festival is not held for the first time in its history. Instead, residents of this darkened city light candles at 9. 03 p. m. expressing their respect to those who died in the defense of Dubrovnik and Croatia.

Sunday, July 12

— Electricity is restored after 38 days.

Monday, July 20

— A ceasefire is agreed to at 10 a. m. with the Yugoslav Army command. It is mediated by the EC monitor mission coordinator in Herceg Novi and Dubrovnik, Colonel David Hepburn.

Compiled by Vesna Čučić

The events which follow are aimed at the implementation of the peace plan proposed by Cyrus Vance which clearly stipulates that the aggressor must withdraw unconditionally from the temporarily occupied regions of the Dubrovnik municipality, from Plat to the Montenegrin border. In this aim, the first meeting between representatives of the Croatian Army and Yugoslav Army is to be held on July 7, 1992, on the boat "Lastovo" southwest of the island of Lokrum. The Yugoslav Army postpones the negotiations which are later held on July 29, 1992, on board the British frigate "Avenger" in international waters south of Dubrovnik. At the talks, the Croatian delegation is led by Croatian Army Commander for the Southern Front, Major General Janko Bobetko. The Yugoslav Army also has negotiators present and the talks are brokered by the EC monitor mission with British General David Cranston and UNPROFOR Deputy Commander Philipe Morillon at the head. An agreement on the unconditional withdrawal of the Serbian–Montenegrin Army from southern Croatia is reached. It is to be done within a short period of time. The agreement is nullified only two or three days before the Yugoslav Army is to start its pull out. Relying upon tried and true methods, representatives of the Yugoslav Army announce that they had not officially signed any document. Therefore, the Dubrovnik region, Konavle and Cavtat with their 3,500 residents, remain occupied. In the meantime, Dubrovnik has been put on general alert once again while sporadic blasts can be heard from a distance. We hope that this dirty war in southern Croatia will nevertheless come to an end soon.

August 1, 1992

According to the agreement concluded in Geneva between the President of the Republic of Croatia, dr. Franjo Tuđman, and Dobrica Ćosić, the President of the Socialist Republic of Yugoslavia, the Yugoslav Army must withdraw from Cavtat, Konavle and Prevlaka area which, according to the Vance plan, was carried out. The peninsula of Prevlaka became a demilitarized zone under the surveillance of UNPROFOR. Thus the south part of Croatia, after more than a year of occupation, became free.

. . .

During the gradual restoration of life and the return of the exiled in the villages and other places of Dubrovnik region which were severely burnt, destroyed and devastated, the Četniks, belonging to the so called Eastern Hercegovina Corps, on February 1993 began to attack again the parts of Konavle, Župa dubrovačka and occasionally the villages in Primorje. From 19 February the attacks became more frequent, their intensity growing all throughout March and a general alarm was announced several times. On 23 March, on Tuesday, after eight months of relative peace, due to the attacks of the enemy from the region of Trebinje, the alarm sounded once again. After that, there was a peaceful period until 14 April, Wednesday, when the region of Konavle was attacked and the alarm sirens were sounded for that area including Župa dubrovačka, but all that ended the same day.

A considerably lengthies chronology of Events has been abridged and edited by Trpimir Macan.

Translated by Kathy Ann Ladun and Ivana Burđelez

Summary of Data Concerning the Human Victims and the Damages to the Buildings and Property During 1991/1992

According to the data collated in the Dubrovnik Museum's department of contemporary history, enemy guns killed 92 civilians and wounded 225 during the most intensive aggression against Dubrovnik and the settlements in the Dubrovnik area in 1991/1992. 129 members of the Croatian Army, of the Ministry of Interior Affairs and the Civilian Guard were killed and 282 wounded defending their own homes and the sovereignty of the Republic of Croatia from the attacks of the Yugoslav Army, the Serbs and Montenegrins. In the same period 361 persons were imprisoned in the enemy camps at Morinj an Bileća, 6 people died as a result of beating and torture.

33,826 banished people, mostly women, children and the elderly from the surroundings of Dubrovnik sought rescue in Dubrovnik from enemy agression. Some of them were taken care of in other parts of Croatia, so that 11,214 banished persons and 892 refugees were living in Dubrovnik by the end of 1992.

By stealthy plunder and the destruction of human lives and natural resources the aggressor damaged a total of 7757 dwellings (1,353,501 m^2 of space)

110

stretching from Konavle to the Ston littoral. 539 buildings were totally burned down, and 1051 buildings were heavily damaged. Numerous static cultural objects (churches, monasteries, cemeteries, museums, local collections, fountains, city walls, etc) were destroyed or heavily damaged, as well as numerous portable monuments of priceless value to the Croatian heritage. The attackers destroyed 750 assorted vessels and 863 vehicles, and they stole 593 cars.

2272 unexploded mines were removed and destroyed from the nearest to the city area (11 km^2). It is estimated that 14,000 shells of various calibre fell in that area.

General Characteristics Concerning the Events of the War between 1993–1995

The events in the period from 1993 to 1995 could be called the second phase of war in the Croatian south. After the breaking of the blockade around Dubrovnik, and liberation of all areas under enemy occupation in the spring, summer and autumn of 1992, there was no complete peace in the broader Dubrovnik area. However, a balance of forces was established, and the Croatian Army secured its positions along the state borders. Only Prevlaka, the most southern part of Croatia was secured by the UN monitors. The attacks on Croatian territory by the Chetniks from East Herzegovina had an essentially different character during this period from the former ones and they were reduced to a terrorist blackmailing of the internationally recognized and sovereing Republic of Croatia. Chetniks were still attacking spasmodically by guns, most often Konavle and the Dubrovnik littoral, while the situation on the border with Montenegro stabilized gradually, but Serbian–Montenegrin pretensions towards Prevlaka were still acute. The repeated attacks by the Chetniks from Herzegovina and their war of destruction culminated between July and September 1995. We can freely say that the immediate danger of war was finished by the outstanding action of the Croatian Army and the police forces under the name of the *Tempest,* at the beginning of August 1995. Peace was secured by the Dayton agreement in November the same year.

The life of Dubrovnik during these three years was characterized by the repairing of damage in the City and in the surroundings, and by the gradual return of the banished people and the refugees. Many European and world state, political, religious and humanitarian organizations excelled, together with the Croatian government, in the reconstruction of the Dubrovnik area, as well as numerous friends of Dubrovnik from the country and from abroad.

Events During 1993

January 9

— The reconstruction of the church of St. Vlaho began; the first major reconstruction attempt in the City.

January 28

— Negotiations between the representatives of the Croatian Ministry of Interior Affairs and Montenegro about the stabilization of peace of the frontier took place in Dubrovnik.

During March

— A series of armed incidents provoked by the Serbians, the soldiers of the so called "Herzegovina corps", occurred at the front line.

April 13

— The Dubrovnik–Neretva county, with its seat in Dubrovnik, was established according to the new territorial and administrative constitution of the Republic of Croatia.

April 21

— After 60 years, the world congress of PEN took place in Dubrovnik for the second time; writers from all over the world condemned the aggression against the City.

June 29

— A fierce mortar attack by the Serbs from Herzegovina on Cavtat. There were no victims but serious material damage was done.

July 5

— The president of Croatia, dr. Tuđman, on the basis of the inviolability of sovereignty, rejected territorial requests by the Serbs from Bosnia and Herzegovina for access to the sea in the region of Konavle. There was no question of an exchange of territory.

During August and September

— Vessels from the Sixth fleet of the USA sailed into Dubrovnik water in connection with military activities in Bosnia and Herzegovina.

During October

— The airport of Dubrovnik was repaired.

— At the beginning of November, work for the systematic reconstruction of all roofs in the old city began.

Events During 1994

— In a period of relative peace and reconstruction, the number of banished people decreased slowly as they started to return and repair, with the help of the state, their destroyed homes in Primorje, Zupa and Konavle. There were 7100 banished persons in July 1993, while 4826 of them were registered at the beginning of July 1994. As infrastructure war first repaired in the devastated areas, 2200 banished persons returned to the less damaged houses in two years time. Others still kept their status of bannished persons. Because of the excellent progress of the reconstruction, all Dubrovnik homeless persons should be able to return under the repaired roofs by the end of 1997.

In May

— The majority of wooden boardings and protective sand bags around the monuments of Dubrovnik and other buildings were removed. Unfortunately, this was done too early in the event so that the treasured monuments of the old city nucleus had to be "shackled" once again.

During July and August

— The Herzegovinian Chetniks several times bombarded the broader area of the Dubrovnik airport so that air traffic was often disrupted.

Events During 1995

From the beginning of April

— Shelling of Konavle, Primorje and the surroundings of the City were frequent. Armed incidents happened almost every ay, and we can only mention the more fierce attacks.

April 13

— Civilian targets in the broader area of Dubrovnik were attacked. The Chetniks sent 21 shells and 8 mortar bombs to Konavle, and they destroyed the fuel reservoir in the airport causing major material damage. 20 missiles fell on Orašac, 3 people were wounded and one killed.

April 25

— The interstate commission had a meeting in Dubrovnik in order to maintain peace at the border. The commission consisted of the representatives of the Croatian Ministry of Interior Affairs, Montenegro and the UN.

May 25

— Strong shelling of Čilipi and the Airport Dubrovnik. A general danger alert was proclaimed for the area of Konavle.

June 14

— Shelling of Močići in Konavle.

During July

— Shelling of Čilipi and the airport from positions near Trebinje happened every day. Stronger attacks occurred on July 4 and 17 when a general danger alert was proclaimed in Konavle.

July 28

— The Herzegovinian Chetniks partly damage the water pipe which supplied Herceg–Novi and its surroundings with water via Konavle. Representatives of Dubrovnik and Herceg–Novi were negotiating regarding the repairing and the further supply of water, in the presence of representatives from the UN.

August 3

— The Herzegovinian Chetniks started shelling Konavle, Župa and the western part of the City surroundings at 6,30 p. m. The general danger alert was sounded for all the attacked places. The treacherous shelling of the Zaton beach killed three young people and wounded 15 civilians, mostly girls and boys who were sun bathing on the shore.

August 4

— The general danger alert was sounded for the confines of the City.

August 5

— The major action of the Croatian Army and the Ministry of Interior Affairs under the name of the *Tempest* began in the early hours. The aim was to liberate those parts of Croatia under the occupation of Serbian rebels. The same morning, a strong shelling attack on the Dubrovnik area began. During the action of the *Tempest,* which was successfully completed on August 8, tension and suspense reigned over the Dubrovnik front. Due to the state of readiness and good weaponry of the Croatian Army, the Chetniks from east

Herzegovina did not dare to threaten the Croatian border but limited their action to long range gun attacks.

August 9

— The suspension of the general danger was proclaimed for the narrower area of Dubrovnik.

August 12

— A strong shelling attack on the whole Dubrovnik area and on the City itself began at 5,30 a. m., and a general danger alert was proclaimed. The repaired city shelters were opened again. The Chetniks launched several hundred missiles ranging between Slano and the south part of Konavle. Some major fires burst out as the consequence of the attacks.

August — 13–16

— The longest Chetniks' attack since 1991. Civilian targets were intensively bombarded as well as the frontline positions of the Croatian Army. The fires provoked by inflammable missiles blazed up in Konavle, Župa and Primorje, as well as in the very vicinity of the City at Srđ. All fire brigades from the Dubrovnik–Neretva and Split–Dalmatian counties were engaged, as well as the members of the fire brigade from the Civilian Guard. 16 persons were wounded up to August 15. The heardquarters of the Civilian Guard postponed the beginning of teaching in schools and work in kindergartens. The Dubrovnik bishop, Monsg. Želimir Puljić celebrated mass in the tower of Revelin during the feast of Our Lady on August 15. The tower of Revelin was the biggest Dubrovnik shelter during the war years. The same day, the chief–of–staff of the Croatian Army, general Zvonimir Červenko emphasized that the Croatian Army would not allow further attacks on the Dubrovnik area and it would do its best to force the suspension of the attacks. The general danger alert for the narrower City area was suspended on August 16, but the protection of monuments and the additional securing of shelters began again as necessary precautions.

August 19

— The president of the Croatian government, Nikica Valentić, came to Dubrovnik and guaranteed to the population of the Dubrovnik area complete security in the very near future.

August — 20–24

— Mortar attacks on the broader Dubrovnik area of lesser intensity continued, so that the general danger alert remained in force.

August 28

— The main director of UNESCO, Frederico Mayor, warned world public opinion that the attacks on Dubrovnik, which was protected by the international convention, are a war crime. Mayor reminded the world of the fact that the committers of such crimes must be responsible to the International Court in the Hague. However, as yet the criminals have not been punished.

Until the End of September

— The general danger alert remained in force for the broader area from Slano to Prevlaka in Konavle due to the minor attacks of the Herzegovian Chetniks.

November 22

— After several days of negotiations among presidents Tudjman, Izetbegovic and Milosevic at the air base Wright–Patterson nea Dayton, and by the mediation of the president of the USA Bill Clinton, complete Croatian–Serbian–Muslim (Bosnian) political agreement was reached. In accordance with its peaceful solution, the Dayton agreement envisaged a considerable part of the Dubrovnik hinterland as belonging to the Federation of Bosnia and Herzegovina, by which the strategic positioin of the whole southern part of the Croatian littoral was essentially improved. The Dayton agreement removed also all the pretensions of the Bosnian Serbs and Montenegrins for part of the Croatian coast, as well as speculations about the exchange of territory. Full Croatian sovereignty within the existing borders was guaranteed again.

Composed by Stjepan Ćosić

Translated by Živan Filippi

PUBLISHER
Matica hrvatska Dubrovnik
Između polača 28, Dubrovnik

FOR THE PUBLISHER
Vlaho Benković

PROOF READING
Ljerka Depolo, Vesna Čučić

COVER PAGE DESIGN AND LAYOUT
Luka Gusić

COMPUTER TYPESETTING
Durieux d. o. o.

PRINTING
Tiskara Puljko, Zagreb

FRONT COVER PHOTO
Damir Viličić: The street Između polača during the fiercest shelling, December 6, 1991

BACK COVER PHOTO
Božo Đukić: Crown of the well in the convent of St. Clara riddled by shrapnels, Autumn 1991

The articles for this edition were written between autumn 1991 and spring 1992. They were published, together with all the photos, in the review "Dubrovnik" under the croatian title "Dubrovnik u ratu".